JUAN CORTINA AND THE TEXAS-MEXICO FRONTIER, 1859-1877

This widely published carte de visite *of Cortina was probably taken in Matamoros a few years after the raid on Brownsville. (Editor's collection)*

JUAN CORTINA AND THE TEXAS-MEXICO FRONTIER
1859-1877

EDITED WITH AN INTRODUCTION
BY JERRY D. THOMPSON

Texas
Western
Press

The University of Texas at El Paso
Southwestern Studies No. 99
1994

First Edition
Library of Congress Catalog No. 92-062469
ISBN 0-87404-195-3

Texas Western Press books are printed on acid-free paper, meeting the guidelines for permanence and durability of the Committee on Production Guidelines
for Book Longevity of the Council on Library Resources.

Cover illustration: Juan Nepomunceno Cortina, 1859 *by José Cisneros.*

Texas Western Press gratefully
acknowledges the grant from
Union National Bank of Texas
which assisted in the publication of this book.

CONTENTS

FOREWORD

Several observations may be made about this collection of documents on the life of Juan Nepomuceno Cortina.

First, it tells of the quality of the forthcoming and long-awaited biography from Jerry D. Thompson's competent research.

Second, it moves us beyond easy caricatures heretofore painted of Cortina; instead, these archival sources disclose the complexity of a man rising to defend the Mexican name in Texas, of the caudillo in Tamaulipas whose tenacity struck terror on competitors, and of the wily politician who survived the tumultuous administrations of Antonio López de Santa Anna, Benito Juárez, Maximilian, Sebastián Lerdo de Tejada, and part of that of Porfirio Díaz.

Lastly, the work underscores the transnational nature of border history, for what transpired in Matamoros and northern Mexico during the Mexican War, the Civil War, the French intervention, and the Cattle Era of the 1860s and 1870s clearly impacted on events in South Texas. The finished tome is destined to rank alongside important biographies currently being written by other historians of the Mexican American experience.

Arnoldo De León
C. J. "Red" Davidson Professor of History
Angelo State University

Introduction

He helped exterminate the last remaining band of Karankawa Indians, shot the Brownsville marshal, ambushed Texas Rangers, captured the United States mail, defeated the Matamoros militia, battled the United States Army, harassed the Confederate Army, ambushed French Imperialists, attacked Mexican liberals, and fought anyone else who dared get in his way. He defied one Mexican president, revolted against a second, and fell victim to the political intrigues of a third. He claimed to be a Mexican patriot, but deserted his nation during its greatest crisis. He never learned to read—and only with difficulty could he write his name—but he rose to political and military heights of which the more literate could only dream.

Born in Camargo, Tamaulipas, on 16 May 1824, he spent his formative years on the north bank of the Río Bravo, participating in the rough-and-tumble politics of Cameron County at the same time he held a commission in the Mexican militia. To many of the desperately poor, politically disfranchised, and economically abused along the river, he was a savior straight from heaven, a high-stepping brush country caudillo who would restore their pride and dignity, abolish the evils of Anglo-American barrister shenanigans, and restore Mexican authority north to the Nueces River and perhaps beyond. At age twenty-two, as a corporal in the Defensores de la Patria, a company of the Guardia Nacional de Tamaulipas, he fought in the battles of Palo Alto and Resaca de la Palma; in the

*Part of the introduction was read as papers at meetings of the Southwestern Council of Latin American Studies (1989), the Texas State Historical Association (1990), and as the O'Connor Lecture at the Conference on South Texas Studies (1991).

three decades that followed, he was in at least thirty other battles and skir-mishes, yet never was wounded. In combat he displayed a bravery and coolness that defied belief, but while most Anglo-Americans remembered him as only a ruthless and brutal bandit who on occasion heartlessly executed his enemies, evidence exists, paradoxically, of his kindness and gentle manners.

Scholars have little doubt that he orchestrated the theft of more cattle in Texas than any man ever, yet he was accused of hundreds of other crimes all the way from Laredo to the Gulf of Mexico, none of which he could have conceivably committed. Like "Old John Brown" of Pottawatomie and Harper's Ferry fame, who rode onto the pages of history at virtually the same time, he was one of the few individuals to be indicted for treason by a state.

As a result of his real and alleged activities, the mere mention of his name in Texas today brings instant recognition from librarians, archivists, and histo-rians. Middle school students read of his daring 1859 Brownsville Raid and his defiance of Texas Rangers and the United States Army. Even today in smoke-filled, Budweiser-cluttered *cantinas* along the border, lively *corridos* recall his daring deeds. But in Mexico, with the exception of the cities of Camargo, Matamoros, and Ciudad Victoria, he has largely been forgotten.

* * * * * * * * * *

His name was Juan Nepomuceno Cortina and he dominated a large part of the nineteenth-century history of the Texas-Mexican frontier. Although he has caught the imagination of a number of prominent historians and novelists, a definitive biography of the man has yet to be written.

Much of what we know about Cortina, especially his early life, has come from that old frontiersman John Salmon Ford. Ford compiled a voluminous set of memoirs that are of great value for those interested in border history. In fact, one of the few physical descriptions of Cortina comes from "Old Rip," who described Cortina as being of "medium size, with regular features and a rather pleasing countenance. He was rather fairer than most men of his nationality. He was fearless, self-possessed, and cunning. In some cases he . . . acted towards personal and political enemies with a clemency worthy of imitation . . . In native intellect [he] ranked high."[1] Ford, who spent six months in 1859 and 1860 and much of 1861 battling Cortina, also referred to the border raider as the "black sheep of the family . . . [who] was bad in school," a bully who would rather fight than learn to read and write, a "marauding chief . . . frontier pirate, notorious champion . . . [and] the Red Robber of the Rio Grande."[2] To Ford, Cortina insti-gated a "predator war . . . [and wrote] his name in blood and fire."[3]

Consequently, much of Cortina's negative image has come line for line from Ford's memoirs. A close reading of the historical record, however, shows that Ford, throughout his life, had a kind of love-hate attitude toward Cortina. Ford's ambiguous feelings toward Cortina probably stem from the friendship Cortina professed toward Ford's wife, Addie, in Matamoros during the Civil War.[4] In turn, Addie's sympathetic treatment may have been a response to Ford's insistence that Cortina's mother not be molested by the Rangers during the First Cortina War. Also of importance is the fact that Ford took credit for saving Cortina's life in 1876 when Pres. Porfirio Díaz ordered Servando Canales, one of Cortina's bitterest enemies, to court-martial Cortina. Ford, however, maintained that Díaz was motivated by a substantial loan from several Brownsville businessmen who wanted Cortina removed from the border; Ford asserted that one of the men who gave Díaz $50,000 to have Cortina arrested was Sabas Cavazos, Cortina's older half-brother.[5] Subsequently, Canales, acting under Díaz's orders, had Cortina tried, and when Cortina was found guilty, Canales ordered him shot. Ford claimed that he personally rushed across the Rio Grande and persuaded Canales to send Cortina to Mexico City where President Díaz could decide his fate.[6] But in addition to American diplomatic pressure, President Díaz's primary reason for removing Cortina from the border was that he could not afford two caudillos vying for power in Tamaulipas at such a crucial time in Mexican history.

Much of what Ford wrote about Cortina during the Cortina Wars reads like high drama. For example, in the Battle at La Bolsa, following Cortina's decisive defeat at Rio Grande City, Ford vividly recalled the final scene: "Cortina was the last to leave the field. He faced his pursuers, emptied his revolver, and tried to halt his panic-stricken men. Lieutenants Dix and Howard and Private George Morris were near Captain Ford. [Ford] ordered them to fire at Cortina. They did so. One shot struck the cantle of his saddle, one cut out a lock of hair from his head, a third cut his bridle rein, a fourth passed through his horse's ear, and a fifth struck his belt. He galloped off unhurt."[7]

Escapades such as these did not escape the pen of renowned Texas folklorist J. Frank Dobie, who had much more than just a passing interest in Cortina. A son of the South Texas brush country himself, Dobie appeared fascinated by Cortina. In his *A Vaquero of the Brush Country*, Dobie refers to Cortina as "the most striking, the most powerful, the most insolent, and the most daring as well as the most elusive Mexican bandit, not even excepting Pancho Villa, that ever wet his horse in the muddy waters of the Río Bravo."[8] Basing his knowledge of Cortina on civil and military depositions taken in Texas, Dobie maintained, however, that Cortina was responsible for a "reign of terror." To Dobie, Cortina was a "great bandido," a "plunderer and murderer."[9] In his final analysis, Dobie's real heroes were not "great bandidos," but instead Capt. L. H. McNelly and his high-stepping Texas Rangers.

One of Dobie's distinguished colleagues passed a slightly less severe judgment on Cortina. The Cortina that emerged in Walter Prescott Webb's *The Texas Rangers* in 1935 was not radically different from Dobie's Cortina, but Webb's portrayal was far more objective in his understanding of the discrimination that existed in Brownsville in the decade after the Mexican War—blatant discrimination that made possible the bloody, ethnic Cortina Wars that were to follow. "Here, indeed," Webb wrote, "was rich soil in which to plant the seed of revolution and race war."[10] Still, even to Webb, Cortina remained a "black sheep," someone who was "impervious to all good influences," an individual who "inherited personal charm . . . flair for leadership . . . [and the] disposition of a gambler."[11]

Webb admits that the Rangers, especially those under Capt. William G. Tobin who arrived in Brownsville in 1859, were "a sorry lot" and were responsible for the hanging of Tomás Cabrera, a sixty-year-old lieutenant of Cortina. This hanging, Webb maintained accurately, helped to generate much of the violence that followed. However, in a line or two without comment, Webb excuses the seemingly indiscriminate hanging of Mexican-Americans by Texas Rangers before and after the fight with some of Cortina's *vaqueros* on the Palo Alto prairie near Brownsville in 1875. Nor is Webb critical of the senseless burning of a number of Mexican *jacales* by the Rangers at Las Cuevas. In the end, then, Webb's heroes were the same as Dobie's—the Texas Rangers.

In 1950, some fifteen years after the appearance of Webb's *Texas Rangers*, Lyman L. Woodman, a retired Air Force major, attempted a biography of Cortina. Entitled *Cortina: Rogue of the Rio Grande*, Woodman's 111-page study, though well written, draws on the same sources as the earlier studies by Dobie and Webb. For Woodman, too, Cortina remained the "Number one Mexican Border bandit of all time . . . [an] extraordinary character . . . [and a] virile man [with a] sinister countenance . . . unhampered by conscience."[12] Woodman's Cortina was "a ruthless belligerent . . . sensuous and cruel . . . [and] a selfish and merciless Robin Hood."[13] And as for scruples, Cortina "had none." Woodman did admit, however, that "for all his rascally and evil ways, Cortina did retain one commendable trait, he had a deep love for his cutthroats."[14] However, Woodman's work, while of some interest, remains a strange combination of history and poorly executed romantic fiction. In a number of highly idealized scenes one can hardly tell where the fictional Cortina leaves off and the real Cortina emerges.

Fortunately for scholars, in 1949 a radically different interpretation of Cortina's life had appeared—a work Woodman evidently had not seen. Charles W. Goldfinch, a student at the University of Chicago, and a son-in-law of the well-known Brownsville attorney José T. Canales (Cortina's older brother's great-great grandson), completed the first scholarly study of Cortina. In *Juan N. Cortina, 1824-1892: A Re-Appraisal*, Goldfinch anticipated much of the reinterpretation of Mexican-American history that would characterize the Chicano movement two decades later. With the help of his father-in-law, who had completed some pioneering work on Cortina himself and who had collected a number of family papers and photographs, Goldfinch was able to trace Cortina's ancestry back to Blas María de la Garza Falcón, his great-great grandfather and the founder of Camargo, as well as his great-grandfather, José Salvador de la Garza, who had been given the Espíritu Santo Grant in 1781.[15] Goldfinch also had access to a number of Cameron County court records and land records not previously used.

Goldfinch observed properly that a conspiracy existed in Brownsville to exaggerate Cortina's raid in order to get Federal troops returned to Fort Brown. He also points out, in defense of Cortina, that "although Cortina had taken the law into his hands, he did not rob and steal when he had the city at his mercy as he certainly would have done had he been a bandit."[16] Two of Cortina's victims in the raid on Brownsville, George Morris and William Peter Neal, Goldfinch writes, were not killed but "dispatched." Goldfinch also minimizes the overall importance of Cortina's defeats at the hands of the United States Army and Texas Rangers at El Ebonal, Rio Grande City, and La Bolsa.

Much of Goldfinch's study of Cortina follows the information gathered by the 1873 Mexican Committee of Investigation that was sent by Pres. Benito Juárez to investigate problems on the border. This investigation was organized in response to a similar commission that had been dispatched to the Rio Grande by the United States Congress the previous year. As historian J. Fred Rippy has noted, however, both commissions were "unfair and inaccurate."[17] Although each gathered a wealth of information, such data must be used with caution and objectivity.

Goldfinch agrees with the Mexican commission that Cortina "had not been involved in cattle stealing but had been the victim of a smear campaign conducted by Texans with ulterior motives."[18] In fact, Goldfinch devoted considerable space to a repudiation of much of the testimony of those who had testified against Cortina, especially individuals living on the south bank of the river. Though there is no doubt that Goldfinch was greatly influenced by Carey McWilliams' *North from Mexico* and the book's overall interpretation of

Mexican American history, Goldfinch indicts McWilliams for a distortion of Cortina's career and character. Goldfinch accused McWilliams of being too dependent on sources north of the border and of an almost total neglect of Mexican primary source material, yet it is difficult to find in Goldfinch's own work more than a dozen footnotes from Mexican sources. Nevertheless, Goldfinch's work was a breath of enlightened scholarship. "To try to make a saint of Cortina," he wrote, "would result in [a] great distortion."[19] Still, Cortina's actions put him "on the side of those whose cause was more humane than that of his opponents," wrote Goldfinch. Cortina had the "courage to stand against tyranny and oppression" and is "entitled to a great deal of admiration."[20]

Later historians, especially during the Chicano regeneracy of the late 1960s and early 1970s, attempted to expand Goldfinch's thesis by arguing that Cortina was a "social bandit," someone who simply reacted to the evils of a racist society that suppressed the Mexican-American socially, economically, and politically. This argument was developed by Pedro Castillo and Albert Camarillo in their *Furia y Muerte: Los Bandidos Chicanos* in 1973.[21] Castillo and Camarillo, in turn, utilized Eric Hobsbaum's *Primitive Rebels: Studies in Archaic Forms of Social Movements in the 19th and 20th Centuries,* which had been published in 1959.[22] The noted Tejano scholar Arnoldo De León, in his *They Called Them Greasers: Anglo Attitudes Towards Mexicans in 19th Century Texas,* also utilized the "social bandit" theory in his interpretation of the Cortina War.[23] Robert J. Rosenbaum, in his *Mexicano Resistance in the Southwest: "The Sacred Right of Self-Preservation,"* (using a subtitle taken from Cortina's 30 September 1859 Rancho del Carmen pronunciamiento), agrees that Cortina rebelled against "gringo law officers whose arrogance rose as Anglo merchants and lawyers increased their inroads in the Valley."[24]

Another contemporary scholar, California sociologist Carlos Larralde, who has done extensive research on Cortina, generally agrees with Goldfinch. Larralde, however, goes one step further in that he sees Cortina as the founder of *La Raza Unida,* a precursor of modern chicanismo who struggled to promote "unity, devotion to . . . community, mutual aid, and brotherly love."[25]

Still another useful study, although certainly not biographical, is a 1972 dissertation at Indiana University by Michael G. Webster entitled "Texas Manifest Destiny and the Mexican Border Conflict, 1865-1880." Plowing fertile ground, the study provided new insights into Cortina in the period after 1865 and was one of the first scholarly studies to use a number of Mexican primary sources.[26]

Similarly, one of the most objective studies of Cortina is a 1987 thesis at the University of Texas at Austin by James Ridley Douglas, "Juan Cortina: El Caudillo de la Frontera."[27] Douglas's thesis is enriched by his use of the fifteen-volume collection of papers, documents, and correspondence of Benito Juárez which was published in 1969 and not utilized by Dobie, Webb, Rippy, Goldfinch, or Woodman.

Douglas agrees that Cortina did indeed strive against "the prejudice that has handicapped Mexicans in the United States." But he did so, Douglas contends, "for the benefit of one Mexican in particular, namely Juan Nepomuceno Cortina."[28] Douglas's Cortina "possessed an extraordinary aptitude for intrigue and manipulation." Although Cortina did resort to cattle stealing, Douglas maintains "that such behavior was not at all unusual among the populace, both Mexican and American, along the Lower Rio Grande."[29] Cortina was no more "evil than the other caudillos of Tamaulipas, he was just more effective at it." Douglas concludes by writing: "Just as the Texans used the courts to take Mexicans' lands or violence to subdue them so did Juan Cortina resort to violence to defend his dignity and rights. Simply put, Juan Cortina behaved more like the wealthy and powerful Anglos of South Texas than most observers have cared to admit. The only thing that made Cortina's activities seem so remarkable was that he was one of the few Mexicans with the temerity to challenge American domination."[30]

However, even Douglas's excellent thesis, as might be expected in a short study, treats certain aspects of Cortina's career with a questionable superficiality. For instance, Douglas has Cortina in April 1865 convincing Col. Santos Benavides, the highest ranking Mexican-American in the Confederate Army, to "abandon the American Civil War and fight against the French."[31] But no evidence exists that Benavides had any intention of going over to the Empire, although shifting political alliances and allegiances on the border became terribly complicated in 1864 and 1865.

Finally, any scholarship on Cortina will need to take advantage of some recent work coming from Mirabel Miró Flaquer of the Universidad Autónoma de Tamaulipas in Ciudad Victoria. This material includes a compilation of the papers of Porfirio Díaz relating to the state of Tamaulipas that sheds new light on the last decade of Cortina's life.[32] These documents do not disagree with Douglas's thesis, but rather add depth to the different trials and tribulations Cortina endured.

* * * * * * * * * *

Today Cortina continues to fascinate writers and students of Texas history. He lives in Larry McMurtry's epic and prize-winning *Lonesome Dove* in the character of Pedro Flores who ran "the best armed ranch in northern Mexico" and who "had more or less held nearly a hundred mile stretch of the border . . . for nearly forty years."[33] In one scene in which two wayward and helpless Irish youths were stranded in northern Mexico near the Rio Grande, somehow looking for Galveston, Capt. W. F. Call warned the Emerald Isle teenagers of Old Pedro: "He ain't a gentle man, and if he finds you tomorrow I expect he'll hang you."[34]

In the character Benito Garza, Cortina lives also in James A. Michener's novel *Texas*. At the end of the Mexican War, Michener has a scene where Benito and his brother, disillusioned with the war and Mexico's humiliating defeat, return to the border and their homes: "As the Garzas approached the Rio Grande before turning east toward Matamoros," Michener writes, "they paused to look across the river into the still-contested Nueces Strip, and resting in their saddles, they reached the brutal conclusion . . . 'there is no chance of turning back the norte-americanos.' But in the depth of their despair they saw a chance for personal salvation and Benito, his mustache dark in the blazing sunlight, phrased their oath: 'The yanquis who try to steal that Strip from us, they'll never know a night of security. Their cattle will never graze in peace . . . they'll pay a terrible price for their arrogance.' "[35]

There is little doubt that Cortina dominated the nineteenth-century history of the Texas-Mexican frontier as did no other individual. As a rugged youth, a determined ranchero, or a soldier on the march, he loved the sun-baked, vast and arid, cactus-infested, bleak savannas of northeastern Mexico and South Texas, yet he spent the last decade of his life in the prison of Santiago Tlatelolco and later under house arrest in the soothing heights of Mexico's great central valley. As he grew old and grey, he yearned to return to Matamoros, the city where he had enjoyed his greatest triumphs and where he had spent much of his life. Yet he died of pneumonia in the small rock and adobe village of Azcapotzalco on the outskirts of Mexico City on 30 October 1894.[36] He was buried with military honors just west of the Hill of the Grasshopper in the Panteón de Dolores, not more than a stone's throw from the Rotonda de los Hombres, the final resting place of Mexico's greatest heroes. Today his long neglected grave is covered with weeds and his tombstone has been vandalized.

Cortina was far from a sacrosanct saint. He was a rugged, fearless, and at times ruthless, frontier caudillo. His enemies feared but respected his daring and determination. Through all the sound and fury that was the history of Texas and Mexico, this remarkable man established his niche in history. Cortina was a hero to his people; his legacy will long remain an integral part of the history of the Texas-Mexican border.

What follows are nine of Cortina's pronunciamientos, all recovered from various archives and period newspapers. Arranged chronologically from 1859 to 1877, they span almost two decades of border history. They depict a fiery and idealistic Brownsville ranchero determined to end the brutalization of Mexicans in Texas in 1859; an emerging border caudillo struggling to hold power in Matamoros; a pompous, long-winded, yet pathetically vain revolutionary caged in Mexico City's Santiago Tlatelolco prison in 1875; a reborn revolutionary ready to take the saddle against Pres. Sebastián Lerdo de Tejada in 1876; and an old veteran breathing one last breath of revolutionary zeal from Matamoros in 1877. Although Cortina learned to write his name only after he became governor of Tamaulipas, the pronunciamientos, nevertheless, all appeared over Cortina's name and were clearly his ideas and were certain to have been dictated by him. Along with a short never-before utilized biography, they provide a rare glimpse into the strengths and weaknesses of one of the border's most fascinating characters.

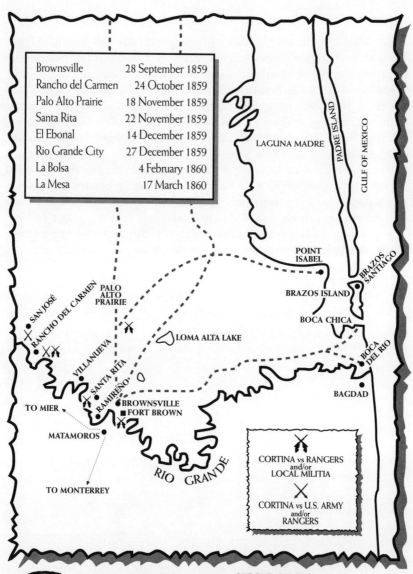

Brownsville	28 September 1859
Rancho del Carmen	24 October 1859
Palo Alto Prairie	18 November 1859
Santa Rita	22 November 1859
El Ebonal	14 December 1859
Rio Grande City	27 December 1859
La Bolsa	4 February 1860
La Mesa	17 March 1860

LAGUNA MADRE

PADRE ISLAND

GULF OF MEXICO

POINT ISABEL

BRAZOS SANTIAGO

BRAZOS ISLAND

BOCA CHICA

SAN JOSÉ

RANCHO DEL CARMEN

PALO ALTO PRAIRIE

LOMA ALTA LAKE

BOCA DEL RIO

VILLANUEVA

SANTA RITA

RAMIREÑO

BROWNSVILLE
FORT BROWN

BAGDAD

TO MIER

MATAMOROS

TO MONTERREY

RIO GRANDE

CORTINA vs RANGERS
and/or
LOCAL MILITIA

CORTINA vs U.S. ARMY
and/or
RANGERS

CORTINA WAR
1859 - 1860

1

In the early morning darkness of 28 September 1859, Juan Nepomuceno Cortina led some seventy-five raiders into the dung-splattered streets of Brownsville, Texas. He was determined to settle a blood feud with a bitter enemy, Adolphus Glavecke. Cortina would also kill or punish other citizens he blamed for murdering Mexicans.

Wielding considerable influence in Cameron County, Glavecke had been elected tax assessor-collector in 1848, county commissioner in 1854, and had served on the city council.[37] A German immigrant, he had arrived on the Rio Grande frontier in 1836 and had married Concepción Ramírez, a widow of Cortina's first cousin.[38] Cortina and Glavecke had known one another for two decades and had rustled cattle and horses together.

In time, Cortina came to mistrust Glavecke, who exerted a Rasputin-like influence over members of Cortina's family—especially Juan's mother, María Estéfana Goseascochea de Cortina. Cortina was especially incensed over the way Glavecke, along with Cameron County Judge Elisha Basse, mishandled and squandered the estate of a deceased aunt, Feliciana Goseascochea.[39] This growing mistrust came to a head in a cattle rustling incident in 1858 in which Glavecke followed Cortina across the river into Mexico to recover cattle stolen from Cameron County.[40] Although both men were indicted in the incident, Cortina swore revenge, and by 1859 he was determined to kill Glavecke on sight.

Another incident leading to the Cortina War came on 13 July 1859, when Cortina rode into Brownsville to Gabriel Catcel's small cafe on Market Square. Looking out on the bustling plaza, he saw the town marshal, Robert Shears, arrest an elderly man who had once worked on his mother's ranch. After giving him a vicious pistol-whipping, Shears was dragging the man off to jail by the collar when Cortina intervened. When the marshal insulted him, Cortina shot the "squinting sheriff," as he called Shears, left him prostrate in the hot and dusty Brownsville street, swung the Mexican up behind him on his horse, and rode out of town to the cheers of a number of Mexicans.[41] In the days that followed, Cortina, largely through offers of monetary compensation, attempted to reconcile his differences with Marshal Shears, but the two could not agree on an exact sum. By September, with indictments pending and no hope of returning to his ranch, Cortina was swearing he would shoot the marshal, too.[42] In the Brownsville raid three months later neither Shears nor Glavecke was killed. Shears managed to conceal himself in an oven, while Glavecke took refuge in a store Cortina was hesitant to enter because of his respect for the owner.

Two men who did die in the Brownsville raid, William Peter Neale and George Morris, had been accused by Cortina of killing Mexicans and going unpunished.[43] Another casualty, town jailer Robert J. Johnson, fell as a result of his refusal to give up the keys to the jail. Johnson had taken refuge in an adjacent store of a friend, Viviano García, and when the raiders rushed García's store, Johnson had killed one of Cortina's men, Alejos Vela. In return, both Johnson and García were killed by the raiders, after which all the prisoners were liberated.[44]

One of the reasons why Cortina, who was in complete control of Brownsville, decided to evacuate the town, as he explains in his pronunciamiento, was the death of the innocent García. No mention is made, however, of the fact that several leading political and military figures from Matamoros had crossed the ferry to persuade him to leave. These included José María Jesús Carvajal, one of the most influential men on the border; Col. Miguel Tijerina, commanding the military in Matamoros and a cousin of Cortina's; Capt. Agapito Longoría; and the Mexican consul, Manuel Treviño.[45]

Cortina's proclamation, a remarkably literate composition, was issued from Rancho del Carmen, his mother's ranch some nine miles upriver from Brownsville, two days after the bloody raid. A well-written defense of his deadly action, the document is addressed to the inhabitants of Texas and especially Brownsville. In the document Cortina clearly views himself as a United States citizen, a matter of some dispute later.

Since Cortina was illiterate at the time, the author of the document remains a mystery, although the ideas expressed are clearly those of Cortina. Speculation has centered around Cortina's well-educated brother, José María.[46] Although he

*William P. Neale died in a hail of bullets during Cortina's September 1859 raid on
Brownsville. Cortina accused Neale and several other men in Brownsville of
killing Tejanos and Mexicanos with impunity. (Editor's photo)*

would later serve his other brother as a colonel in the Mexican military and as a courier to Pres. Benito Juárez, José María, who had been elected tax assessor-collector in Cameron County in 1856, was considered at the time an upstanding and respected member of the Brownsville establishment.[47] He did not ride with his brother on the fateful night of 28 September, but did become involved in the guerrilla war that followed. Others have speculated that the author may have been a member of the Balli family, perhaps Jesús, one of the raiders, or Francisco, who later commanded Cortina's captured artillery. Another possibility, according to Richard Fitzpatrick, the American commercial agent in Matamoros, was a man in Matamoros named Miguel Peña.[48] Such may have been the case since it was well-known that Cortina was supported by a number of influential and well-educated citizens of the town.

The proclamation was printed in Brownsville and circulated on both sides of the river.[49] The only original known to exist today is in the National Archives in Washington, D.C. Although it is in English, the pronunciamiento was certain to have also been printed in Spanish.

* * * * * * * * *

PRONUNCIAMIENTO

Rancho del Carmen

30 September 1859

Juan Nepomuceno Cortinas to the inhabitants of the State of Texas, and especially to those of the city of Brownsville.

An event of grave importance, in which it has fallen to my lot to figure as the principal actor since the morning of the 28th instant, doubtless keeps you in suspense with regard to the progress of its consequences. There is no need of fear. Orderly people and honest citizens are inviolable to us in their persons and interests. Our object as you have seen, has been to chastise the villainy of our enemies, which heretofore has gone unpunished. These have connived with each other, and form, so to speak, a perfidious inquisitorial lodge to persecute and rob us, without any cause, and for no other crime on our part than that of being of Mexican origin; considering us, doubtless, destitute of those gifts which they themselves do not possess.

To defend ourselves, and making use of the sacred right of self-preservation, we have assembled in a popular meeting with a view of discussing a means by which to put an end to our misfortunes.

Our identity of origin, our relationship, and the community of our sufferings, has been, as it appears, the cause of our embracing, directly, the proposed object which led us to enter your beautiful city, clothed with the imposing aspect of our exasperation.

The assembly organized, and headed by your humble servant, (thanks to the confidence which he inspired as one of the most aggrieved), we have careered over the streets of the city in search of our adversaries, inasmuch as justice, being administered by their own hands, the supremacy of the law has failed to accomplish its object.

Some of them, rashly remiss in complying with our demand, have perished for having sought to carry their animosity beyond the limits allowed by their precarious position. Three of them have died—all criminal, wicked men, notorious among the people for their misdeeds. The others, still more unworthy and wretched, dragged themselves through the mire to escape our anger, and now, perhaps, with their usual bravado, pretend to be the cause of an infinity of evils, which might have been avoided but for their cowardice. They concealed themselves, and we were loth to attack them within the dwellings of others, fearing that their cause might be confounded with that of respectable persons, as at last, to our sorrow, did happen. On the other hand, it behooves us to maintain that it was unjust to give the affair such a terrible aspect, and to represent it as of a character foreboding evil; some having carried their blindness so far as to implore the aid of Mexico, alleging as a reason that their persons and property were exposed to vandalism. Were any outrages committed by us during the time we had possession of the city, when we had it in our power to become the arbiters of its fate? Will our enemies be so blind, base, or unthinking, as to deny the evidence of facts? Will there be one to say that he was molested, or that his house was robbed or burned down?

The unfortunate Viviano García fell a victim to his generous behavior; and with such a lamentable occurrence before us on our very outset, we abstained from our purpose, horrified at the thought of having to shed innocent blood without even the assurance that the vile men whom we sought would put aside their cowardice to accept our defiance.

These, as we have said, form, with a multitude of lawyers, a secret conclave, with all its ramifications, for the sole purpose of despoiling the Mexicans of their lands and usurp[ing] them afterwards. This is clearly proven by the conduct of one Adolph Glavecke, who, invested with the character of deputy sheriff, and in collusion with the said lawyers, has spread terror among the unwary, making them believe that he will hang the Mexicans and burn their ranchos, etc., that by this means he might compel them to abandon the country, and thus accomplish their object. This is not a supposition—it is a reality; and notwithstanding the want of better proof—if their threat were not publicly known, all would feel persuaded that of this, and even more, are capable such criminal men as the one last mentioned, the Marshal, the jailor, Morris, Neale, etc. The first of these, in his history and behavior, has ever been infamous and traitorous. He is the assassin of the ill-starred Colonel [Trueman] Cross, Captain Woolsey, and Antoni[o] Mireles, murdered by him at the Rancho de las Prietas, the theatre of all his assassinations.* It is he who instigated some, and aiding others, has been the author of a thousand misdeeds; and to put down the finger of scorn that ever points at him, and do away with the witnesses of his crimes, he has been foremost in persecuting us to death. The others are more or less stamped with ignominy, and we will tolerate them no longer in our midst, because they are obnoxious to tranquility and to our own welfare.

---

*On 21 April 1846, Colonel Cross and Captain Woolsey were killed northwest of Fort Texas (Brown), not far from Rancho del Carmen, by "Mexican bandits" allegedly led by Ramón Falcón. Cross was said to have been on his way to visit a lady friend. Woolsey does not appear in military records of the era. Falcón may be the same man who served in the Union Army as a first lieutenant and who died of disease at Baton Rouge, Louisiana, in January 1865.

All truce between them and us is at an end, from the fact alone of our holding upon this soil our interests and property. And how can it be otherwise, when the ills that weigh upon the unfortunate republic of Mexico have obliged us for many heart-touching causes to abandon it and our possessions in it, or else become the victims of our principles or of the indigence to which its intestine disturbances had reduced us since the treaty of Guadalupe? When, ever diligent and industrious, and desirous of enjoying the longed for boon of liberty within the classic country of its origin, we were induced to naturalize ourselves in it and form a part of the Confederacy, flattered by the bright and peaceful prospect of living therein and inculcate in the bosoms of our children a feeling of gratitude towards a country beneath whose aegis we would have wrought their felicity and contributed with our conduct to give evidence to the whole world that all the aspirations of the Mexicans are confined to one only—*that of being freemen*; and that, having secured this ourselves, those of the old country, notwithstanding their misfortunes, might have nothing to regret save the loss of a section of territory, but with the sweet satisfaction that their old fellow citizens lived therein, enjoying tranquility, as if Providence had so ordained to set them an example of the advantages to be derived from public peace and quietude; when, in fine, all has been but the baseless fabric of a dream, and our hopes having been defrauded in the most cruel manner in which disappointment can strike, there can be found no other solution to our problem than to make one effort, and at one blow destroy the obstacles to our prosperity.

It is necessary: the hour has arrived. Our oppressors number but six or eight. Hospitality and other noble sentiments shield them at present from our wrath, and such, as you have seen, are inviolable to us.

Innocent persons shall not suffer, no; but, if necessary, we will lead a wandering life, awaiting our opportunity to purge society of men so base that they degrade it with their opprobrium. Our families have returned as strangers to their old country to beg for an asylum. Our lands, if they are to be sacrificed to the avaricious covetousness of our enemies, will be rather so on account of our own vicissitudes. As to land, nature will always grant us sufficient to support our frames, and we accept the consequences that may arise. Further, *our personal enemies shall not possess our lands until they have fattened it* (sic) *with their own gore.*

We cherish the hope, however, that the government, for the sake of its own dignity, and in obsequiousness to justice, will accede to our demand, by prosecuting those men and bringing them to trial or leave them to become subject to the consequences of our immutable resolve.

It remains for me to say that, separated as we are, by accident alone, from the other citizens of the city, and not having renounced our rights as North American citizens, we disapprove, and energetically protest, against the act of having caused a force of the National Guards from Mexico to cross unto this side to ingraft themselves in a question so foreign to their country that there is no excusing such weakness on the part of those who implored their aid.

JUAN NEPOMUCENO CORTINAS

September 30th, 1859

2

In the two months since his first pronunciamiento Cortina had gathered a small army of angry Mexicans and had virtually isolated Brownsville from the outside world. He had seized the United States mail and sent the town into a state of panic and despair.

Leading Brownsville citizens Mifflin Kenedy, José San Ramón, and the mayor, Stephen Powers, had formed a Committee of Safety for protection. Besieged and fearful of a second attack, the citizens erected barricades in the streets and posted sentinels day and night. Realizing that any help was hundreds of miles away and weeks in coming, the Committee of Safety asked for assistance from Matamoros.[50] In response, Matamoros authorities sent a company of fifty militia across the river to help defend the town. Brownsville residents watched in awe as Mexican soldiers crossed the Rio Grande to Texas to protect United States citizens from an irregular army of Mexicans being led by a man who considered himself a United States citizen and who had once been a member of the Matamoros militia that now came to protect his enemies. In Austin and Washington it all seemed very confusing.

The Committee of Safety also scribbled out a petition to Gov. Richard Hardin Runnels pleading for protection.[51] Copies were sent to Gen. David E. Twiggs, commanding the 8th Military Department in San Antonio, and to Pres. James Buchanan. With every able-bodied man under guard day and night and "nearly worn down with fatigue," the citizens asked for "prompt, ample, and efficient" protection.[52] With no American soldier within 240 miles, except for ten men on Brazos Santiago, the Committee of Safety wanted federal troops back on the

CORTINA WAR
LOWER RIO GRANDE VALLEY

border. They still appeared dazed at how "a single Mexican outlaw" at the head of "several hundred desperate, lawless, and licentious beings," could hold an entire region of the Lone Star State in his grasp.[53]

From Rancho del Carmen on 5 October 1859, Cortina, with two hundred men, crossed the river into Mexico and rode into Matamoros where he was cheered as a conquering hero.[54] With Cortina back in Mexico, the crisis on the Rio Grande might well have faded into history had not another incident stoked the coals of racial animosity. Early on the morning of 12 October, with Cortina still in Matamoros, a posse led by Sheriff James Browne, once a friend of Cortina's, rode upriver toward Rancho del Carmen where they captured sixty-year-old Tomás Cabrera, recognized from the 28 September raid as Cortina's chief lieutenant. Cabrera was brought into town and thrown in jail.[55]

Within hours of Cabrera's arrest, Cortina approached a number of the "most influential men" in Matamoros and insisted they warn the authorities in Brownsville that if Cabrera were not released, he would "lay the town in ashes."[56] When his demand was refused, he crossed the river with forty of his men and took up defenses again at Rancho del Carmen.

Overly confident, the Committee of Safety decided on 23 October to take the offensive and drive Cortina back into Mexico. Composed of twenty militiamen calling themselves the "Brownsville Tigers," forty poorly-armed Cameron County Mexican rancheros, and the reinforced seventy-five-man Matamoros militia (along with two small four-pounder cannon), the small army marched out of Brownsville and headed upriver for Cortina's camp. Near Rancho del Carmen, Cortina routed the Brownsville Tigers and their allies, took their cannon, and sent the small army fleeing back to Brownsville in panic.[57]

Maj. Samuel P. Heintzelman, who later arrived on the border with the United States Army, put it best when he summarized Cortina's position at this time: "Cortina was now a great man: he had defeated the 'Gringo,' and his position was impregnable; he had the Mexican flag flying in his camp, and numbers were flocking to his standard. When he visited Matamoros, he was received as the champion of his race—as the man who would right the wrongs the Mexicans had received; that he would drive back the hated Americans to the Nueces, and some even spoke of the Sabine as the future boundary."[58]

By the first week of November 1859, news of the "Cortina War" had spread north across the Nueces to San Antonio, Austin, and to the halls of Washington. Texans, already alarmed by news of John Brown's raid on Harper's Ferry, Virginia, and with the press exaggerating Cortina's every move, envisioned an army of little brown-skinned, sombrero-crowned, machete-wielding Nat Turners marching north from the border spreading terror throughout the Lone

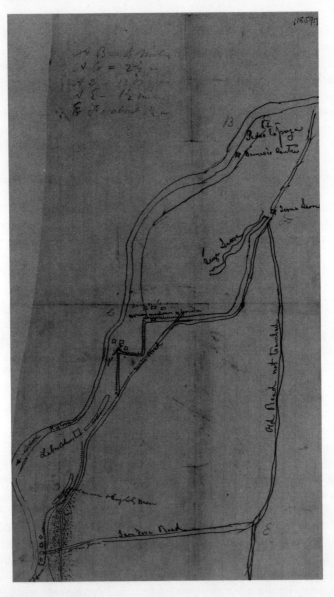

Assisted by Edmund J. Davis, district judge and future governor of Texas, Maj. Samuel Peter Heintzelman carefully sketched Cortina's fortifications before the attack at El Ebonal on 14 December 1859. (Library of Congress)

Star State. A few Anglo-Texans still retained bitter racial recollections of another Mexican army that had marched across the Rio Grande in 1836.

Cortina's second proclamation on 23 November 1859, issued again from his camp at Rancho del Carmen, emphasized many of the same ideas as his first. The loss of land by Mexicans, either through legal manipulation and chicanery or through threats and intimidation, must be avenged, he wrote. The impunity with which Anglos had killed Mexicans in Brownsville and Cameron County must not go unanswered. Furthermore, he stressed that the arrogance of Anglo-American racism must stop.[59]

Now more confident and aware of a much larger audience, Cortina clearly saw himself as the spokesman for all "Mexican Inhabitants of the State of Texas." At the same time, there is a strange and tragic fatalism about his hints at having to enter a "wandering life," and the realization that he might well be on his way to becoming a sacrificial lamb to the happiness of his people.[60]

The pronunciamiento was published in Spanish in Matamoros. It was later translated and reprinted, with a lengthy criticism, probably in the office of the Brownsville *American Flag* as a broadside on 26 November 1859.[61] The broadside referred to Cortina as an "arch-murderer and robber" and a "Christian Comanche." According to the *American Flag*, the pronunciamiento was little more than a "collection of balderdash and impudence." Nevertheless, Cortina had "banded together an imposing army," most of them citizens of Mexico, who were "levying war against the State and Union," and "flying a foreign flag . . . on American soil."[62]

Originals of both the pronunciamiento and the broadside are in the Adjutant General's Records at the National Archives in Washington, D.C.

* * * * * * * * * *

PRONUNCIAMIENTO
Rancho del Carmen
23 November 1859

JUAN N. CORTINA,
To the Mexican Inhabitants of the STATE OF TEXAS!!!

COMPATRIOTS: A sentiment of profound indignation, the love and esteem which I profess for you, the desire which you have for that tranquility and those guarantees which are denied you, thus violating the most sacred laws, is that which moves me to address you these words, hoping that they may prove some consolation in the midst of your adversity, which heretofore has borne the appearance of predestination.

The history of great human actions teaches us that in certain instances the principal motive which gives them impulse teaches the natural right to resist and conquer our enemies with a firm spirit and living will; to persist in, and to reach the consummation of this object, opening a path through the obstacles which step by step are encountered, however imposing or terrible they may be.

In the series of such actions, events present themselves which public opinion, influenced by popular sentiment, calls for deliberation upon their effects, to form an exact and just conception of the interests which they promote; and this same public opinion should be considered as the best judge, which, with coolness and impartiality, does not fail to recognize some principle as the cause for the existence of open force and immutable firmness, which impart the noble desire of cooperating with the true philanthropy to remedy the state of despair of him who, in his turn, becomes the victim of ambition, satisfied at the cost of justice.

There are doubtless persons so overcome by strange prejudices—men without confidence or courage to face danger in an undertaking in sisterhood with the love of liberty, who, examining the merit of acts by a false light, and preferring that of the same opinion contrary to their own, prepare no other reward than that pronounced for the "bandit,"—for him who, with complete abnegation of self, dedicates himself to constant labor for the happiness of those who, suffering under the weight of misfortunes, eat their bread, [and] mingled with tears. If, my dear compatriots, I am honored with the name, I am ready for the combat.

The Mexicans who inhabit this wide region, some because they were born therein, others because since the treaty Guadalupe Hidalgo, they have been attracted to its soil by the soft influence of wise laws and the advantages of a free government, paying little attention to the reasonings of politics, are honorable and exclusively dedicated to the exercise of industry, guided by that instinct which leads the good man to comprehend, as uncontradictory truth, that only in the reign of peace can he enjoy, without inquietude, the fruit of his labor. These, under an unjust imputation of selfishness and churlishness, which do not exist, are not devoid of those sincere and expressive evidences of such friendliness and tenderness as should gain for them that confidence with which they have inspired those who have met them in social intercourse. This genial affability seems as the foundation of that proverbial prudence which as an oracle is consulted in all their actions and undertakings. Their humility, simplicity, and docility, directed with dignity, it may be that with excess of goodness, can, if it be desired, lead them beyond the common class of men, but causes them to excel in an irresistible inclination towards ideas of equality, a proof of their simple manners, so well adapted to that which is styled the classic land of liberty. A man, a family and a people, possessed of qualities so eminent, with their heart in their hand and purity of their lips, encounter every day renewed reasons to know that they are surrounded by malicious and crafty monsters, who rob them in the tranquil interior of home, or with open hatred and pursuit; it necessarily follows, however great may be their pain, if not abased by humiliation and ignominy, their groans suffocated and hushed by a pain which renders them insensible, they become resigned to suffering before an abyss of misfortunes.

Mexicans! When the State of Texas began to receive the new organization which its sovereignty required as an integral part of the Union, flocks of vampires in the guise of men, came and scattered themselves in the settlements, without any capital except the corrupt heart and the most perverse intentions. Some, brimful of laws, pledged to us their protection against the attacks of the rest; others assembled in shadowy councils attempted and excited the robbery and burning of the houses of our relatives on the other side of the river Bravo; while others, to the abusing of our unlimited confidence, when we intrusted them with our titles, which secured the future of our families, refused to return them under false and frivolous pretexts—all, in short, with a smile on their faces, giving the lie to that which their black entrails were meditating. Many of you have been robbed of your property, incarcerated, chased, murdered, and hunted like wild beasts, because your labor was fruitful, and because your industry excited the vile avarice which led them. A voice infernal said, from the bottom of their soul, "Kill them! the greater will be our gain!" Ah! this does not finish the sketch of your situation. It would appear that justice had fled from this world, leaving you to the caprice of your oppressors, who become each day more furious towards you, that, through witnesses and false charges, although the grounds may be insufficient, you may be interred in the penitentiaries, if you are not previously deprived of life by some keeper who covers himself from responsibility by the pretence of your flight. There are to be found criminals covered with frightful crimes, but they appear to have impunity until opportunity furnish them a victim; to these monsters indulgence is shown, because they are not of our race, which is unworthy, as they say, to belong to the human species. But this race, which the Anglo-American, so ostentatious of its own qualities, tries so much to blacken, depreciate, and load with insults, in a spirit of blindness, which goes to the full extent of such things so common on this frontier, does not fear, placed even in the midst of its very faults, those subtle inquisitions which are so frequently made as to its manners, habits, and sentiments; nor that its deeds should be put to the test of examination in the land of reason, of justice, and of honor. This race has never humbled itself before the conqueror, though the reverse has happened, and can be established; for he is not humbled who uses among his fellowmen those courtesies which humanity prescribes, charity being the root whence springs the rule of his actions. But this race, which you see filled with gentleness and inward sweetness, gives now the cry of alarm throughout the entire extent of the land which it occupies, against all the artifice interposed by those who have become chargeable with their division and discord. This race, adorned with the most lovely disposition towards all that is good and useful in the line of progress, omits no acts of diligence which might correct its many imperfections, and lift its grand edifice among the ruins of the past, respecting the ancient traditions and the maxims bequeathed by their ancestors, without being dazzled by brilliant and false appearances, nor crawling to the exaggeration of [an] institution which, like a sublime statue, is offered for their worship and adoration.

Mexicans! Is there no remedy for you? Inviolable laws, yet useless, serve, it is true, certain judges and hypocritical authorities, cemented in evil and injustice to do whatever suits them and to satisfy their vile avarice at the cost of your patience and suffering, rising in their frenzy even to the taking of life, through the treacherous hands of their bailiffs. The wicked way in which many of you have been oftentimes involved in persecutions, accompanied by circumstances making it the more bitter, is now well known; these crimes being hid from society under the shadow of a horrid night, those implacable people, with the haughty spirit which suggests impunity for a life of criminality, have pronounced, doubt ye not, your sentence, which is, with accustomed insensibility, as you have seen, on the point of execution.

Mexicans! My part is taken; the voice of revelation whispers to me that to me is entrusted the work of breaking the chains of your slavery, and that the Lord will enable me with powerful arm to fight against our enemies, in compliance with the requirements of that Sovereign Majesty, who from this day forward, will hold us under His protection. On my part, I am ready to offer myself as a sacrifice for your happiness; and counting upon the means necessary for the discharge of my ministry, you may count upon my cooperation, should no cowardly attempt put an end to my days.

This undertaking will be sustained on the following bases:

FIRST. A society is organized in the State of Texas, which devotes itself sleeplessly, until the work is crowned with success, to the improvement of the unhappy condition of those Mexicans residents therein; exterminating their tyrants, to which end those which compose it are ready to shed their blood and suffer the death of martyrs.

SECOND. As this society contains within itself the elements necessary to accomplish the great end of its labors, the veil of impenetrable secrecy covers "The Great Book" in which the articles of its constitution are written; while so delicate are the difficulties which must be overcome that no honorable man can have

cause for alarm if imperious exigencies require them to act
without reserve.

THIRD. The Mexicans of Texas repose their lot under the good
sentiments of the governor elect of the State, General Houston,
and trust that upon his elevation to power he will begin with care
to give us legal protection within the limits of his powers.

Mexicans! Peace be with you! Good inhabitants of State of
Texas, look on them as brothers, and keep in mind that which the
Holy Spirit saith: "Thou shalt not be the friend of the passionate
man; nor join thyself to the madman, lest thou learn his mode of
work and scandalize thy soul."

County of Cameron
Camp at the Rancho del Carmen, November 23, 1859

JUAN N. CORTINAS

3

Juan N. Cortina's rise to power in Tamaulipas was indirectly related to the American Civil War and the arrival of the Federal Army on the Rio Grande in November 1863. Through the clever and cunning American consul in Matamoros, Leonard Pierce, Jr., Cortina had made contact with Federal authorities in New Orleans. The Union Army had even gone so far as to ship ammunition and supplies to pro-Cortina guerrillas operating from bases in Mexico against the Confederate Army in South Texas.[63] From Matamoros, Cortina had written John L. Haynes, now a colonel in the Texas Union Army and one of the few Anglos in Texas to rationalize Cortina's 1859 Brownsville Raid. Cortina pledged his cooperation should the Federal army occupy the left bank of the Rio Grande.[64]

Five months after the battles of Gettysburg and Vicksburg, on 2 November 1863, from the flagship *McClellan* off Brazos Santiago, Gen. Nathaniel P. Banks, commanding the Union Rio Grande Expedition, sent a simple message to Washington: "The flag of the Union floated over Texas today at meridian precisely."[65] Banks had steamed with some 6,998 Union soldiers that included five regiments of Midwestern farm boys, a regiment from distant Maine, two regiments of the black Corps d'Afrique, and a cavalry contingent of Texas Unionists.[66] The Union Army had come from New Orleans through a terrible storm to cut the lucrative Texas cotton trade and to show the Stars and Stripes to the French in Mexico.

At midmorning on 6 November, with flags flapping in the breeze and dazed townspeople looking on, the 94th Illinois Volunteers, vanguard of Banks' army in blue, entered Brownsville to be followed within hours by the 1st Missouri Artillery and the 13th Maine Volunteers.[67] Arriving in town the same day, General Banks turned his attention to the situation in Matamoros and to Cortina, who was now a lieutenant colonel. According to Banks, the emerging caudillo was "thoroughly hostile to the French interests."[68] Although "an uneducated man, and of not very prepossessing manners," Cortina was nevertheless of great influence with the populace on both sides of the river, Banks wrote.[69] "His friends count him as in the interests of the United States Government, and we have relied upon his assistance in raising Mexican troops," Banks continued.[70]

Upon arriving in Brownsville, the Union Army found part of the town in ruins, Fort Brown in ashes, sacked and plundered stores, and a frightened populace. The chaos had started four days earlier, at 3 A.M. on the morning of 2 November 1863, when Brig. Gen. Hamilton P. Bee, commanding fewer than 150 Confederates in Brownsville, had heard that the Federal fleet was off the coast.[71] The baby-faced Bee had hastily sent patrols to Point Isabel and to the mouth of the Rio Grande to verify the news. One of General Bee's officers, Capt. Richard Taylor, had subsequently verified this activity: "Brazos Island is covered with tents; six regimental flags were counted; twenty-six vessels, some of them very large."[72] Realizing any resistance would be senseless, Bee then ordered most of the commissary and quartermaster stores at Fort Brown destroyed and the post burned. All the cotton that could not be transported north was set on fire or thrown in the river. A strong wind carried the sparks and smoke into the town and an entire block of buildings near the ferry was soon in flames. Some eight thousand pounds of powder in the fort magazine exploded, adding even more terror to an already frightened populace: "Peril was around me on all sides," Bee wrote Confederate headquarters in Houston.[73] With clouds of smoke billowing skyward, the town in panic, his men deserting, and the Federal Army advancing, General Bee bid a boozy farewell to the Rio Grande and led a large wagon train north for the King Ranch and the Nueces River.

With violence and disorder everywhere, Judge Israel Bigelow, in a strange reversal of fortunes since 1859, sent an urgent plea to Lieutenant Colonel Cortina in Matamoros for help, but Cortina replied that Bigelow's problems were not his and refused to intervene. Instead, a forty-five-year-old bandit chief and former officer in the Mexican Army, Gen. José María Cobos, stepped forward. With two hundred hastily-recruited men, Cobos was able to stop the plunder and restore some semblance of order.[74] Active earlier with the conservatives in Coahuila and Zacatecas, but expelled from Mexico, Cobos had been in Brownsville hoping to procure American arms and ammunition, recruit men, and seize Matamoros. Probably through Leonard Pierce, Jr., the reactionary

Cobos had made contact with Cortina, and the two had agreed to cooperate in ousting the military governor, Manuel Ruiz.

Before daybreak on 6 November with Union forces approaching Brownsville, Cobos crossed the river to Matamoros and with Cortina's help, seized the town from the Juarista Ruiz. Cortina not only helped Cobos take Matamoros, but consented to Cobos' becoming governor of Tamaulipas while he would become head of the ayuntamiento or common council and remain as military commander.[75] On the same day, Cobos issued a pronunciamiento to his soldiers, saying that he had come to save them from anarchy; he spoke of independence and patriotism but appeared ambiguous about any allegiance to the French.[76] But despite Cobos' public anti-French protestations, he was really a friend of the Empire and "a desperate man," General Banks wrote.[77] When the Spanish-born Cobos assailed the liberal constitution of 1857, and criticized "the accumulation of outrages" thrust upon the people of Mexico by a "tyrannical demagogue," Benito Juárez, Cortina, too, saw the pronunciamiento as a clear sign of allegiance to the French.

On 7 November, only one day after he seized power, Governor Cobos and Lt. Gov. Rómulo Vila ordered Ruiz executed. Cortina instead vetoed the plan and had Cobos and Vila arrested, summoned before a hastily called court-martial, and when the two were quickly found guilty, ordered them shot. At 8 A.M. on 7 November, with a large part of the Matamoros populace looking on, Cobos was taken to the outskirts of town near a lagoon and executed by a platoon of Cortinistas. Vila, also a Spaniard, was allowed to "run the gauntlet, and was shot upon his flight."[78] Ruiz was immediately released and offered a guard of twenty-five men to insure "his retreat from the city."[79] Not trusting Cortina, and fearing that he, too, would be executed, Ruiz crossed the river to Brownsville to seek the protection of General Banks.

Within days, Cortina called for the return of Jesús de la Serna, a Juarista who had been elected governor in 1861. In the violent and complicated world of Tamaulipas politics, Serna in time would lose out also, and Cortina would become the de facto governor of Tamaulipas.

In Cortina's 8 November 1863 pronunciamiento that follows, the caudillo sets out to explain to the fifteen thousand citizens of Matamoros his reasons for executing Cobos. On the same day the pronunciamiento was issued, General Banks sent a copy to Maj. Gen. Henry W. Halleck in Washington. The original copy, reprinted in the *Official Records of the Union and Confederate Armies*, is at the National Archives.[80]

* * * * * * * * * *

PRONUNCIAMIENTO

Matamoros

8 November 1863

To the Public:

The subscriber, feeling himself obliged to explain promptly to the nation, as well as the people of this heroic city and the armed garrison which he has the honor to command, the reason for the execution done at 8 o'clock yesterday morning on the person of Don José M. Cobos, and as neither time nor the demands of the service to which he is preeminently dedicated in order to maintain tranquility and order among the people will permit him to make an elaborate explanation of what has taken place, he will merely say that the garrison agreed to proclaim the raising of the siege in Tamaulipas, thereby re-establishing constitutional order, as the situation was no longer endurable in the state, for reasons which he proposes to explain to the Supreme Government of the nation. Cobos assented to this idea, and, under its protection, he was able, only in appearance, to obtain the command of the soldiers, including him who subscribes himself their chief, all being Mexicans, belonging to the country, and, as Liberals, they are disposed to sacrifice themselves to sustain and protect the constitution of 1857, no less than the Government from which it emanates. He then made the first step toward discord, issuing a proclamation, in which he could not avoid showing the tendency of his ideas, contrary to the fundamental letter of the Republic, and of the legitimate Government established by virtue of it, crowning the work which he proposed to erect in Tamaulipas with the abortion of a plan, which, reduced to writing and signed, should take the place of that. What madness!

At this state of things it was necessary to work as became the defenders of the code of 1857. Consequently Cobos was shot. As for the rest, the garrison, with the people and the first ayuntamiento (common council) of this heroic city, have done away with the proclamation by raising the siege, and the consequent result by changing the face of the State, purely with the feeling that it enters and inhabitants will have the guarantees stipulated by law, to whose preservation I have consecrated the arms of the faithful soldiery which are subservient to me.

JUAN NEPOMUCENO CORTINA

4

Shortly after Cortina's seizure of power in Matamoros in early November 1863 and the subsequent flight of Gov. Manuel Ruiz to Brownsville, the deposed governor rode upriver, recrossed the Rio Grande and proceeded to San Fernando, south of Matamoros, where he began to build an army.[81] By early December, Ruiz had recruited six hundred men and was preparing to drive Cortina out of Brownsville. Meanwhile, in Matamoros, Cortina had barricaded the streets with Texas cotton and was braced for an attack.[82] By 11 December, Maj. Gen. N.J.T. Dana, commanding the Union forces in Brownsville, reported that Matamoros was in a "great panic and confusion . . . and an attack hourly expected."[83] But one week later Ruiz was still at San Fernando.[84]

By early January 1864, Ruiz finally arrived on the outskirts of Matamoros to demand the surrender of the town; a bloody confrontation appeared imminent. At first Cortina seemed determined to fight, and civilians, including Cortina's own family, were evacuated to Brownsville. He finally agreed, however, to negotiate and sent an emissary to meet with representatives of Governor Ruiz.[85] At a tense parley on the outskirts of Matamoros, it was decided that Governor Serna, a Cortina supporter, would again retire to private life, Ruiz would take his seat as governor, and Cortina and Ruiz would combine their armies into a single fighting force. Gen. José Macedonio Capistrán, a Ruiz man, would head the army while Cortina would be second in command. Leaving Ruiz in Matamoros, the army would then march against the French at Tampico.[86]

Serna retired to his ranch, Ruiz took his seat as governor, and the soldiers prepared to move out. But Cortina hesitated in marching for Tampico.[87] After five days, with the Cortinistas still refusing to leave, Ruiz sent a messenger to inquire as to why Cortina was not on the road. Cortina replied that his men had not been paid, then when the men were given two months' pay, Cortina demanded four hundred horses and more ammunition.[88] During this time, a Union officer in Brownsville recorded in his diary that Cortina's men "loitered through the city with an easy nonchalance [while] . . . officers rode through the streets with bravado stamped on every action."[89]

But trouble was brewing. On the afternoon of 12 January 1864, one of Cortina's officers, Col. Octaviano Cárdenas, rode up to the house where Governor Ruiz was staying and allegedly insulted the governor, even shouting "death to Ruiz."[90] Cárdenas was seized by the governor's guards, carried into a back yard, and shot within thirty minutes.

Less than three hours later, with Cortina vowing revenge, the two armies opened fire on one another in a fierce artillery duel near the main plaza; Cortina had six hundred men and six artillery pieces, while Ruiz had eight hundred men and four artillery pieces.[91] The fighting continued through the night and into the next day with as many as 250 artillery rounds being exchanged. The American consul in Matamoros, Leonard Pierce, Jr., was panic-stricken: "A battle is now raging in the streets of this city," he wrote.[92] "My person and family are in great danger, as the road between here and the ferry is said to be infested with robbers. I have also about $1,000,000 in specie and a large amount of other valuable property under my charge in the consulate, and from the well-known character of Cortina and his followers, I fear the city will be plundered."[93] Pierce asked Maj. Gen. Francis J. Herron, now commanding the Federal forces in Brownsville, to intervene "at the earliest possible moment," to save his family and carry the specie to Brownsville.[94]

At the same time, Governor Ruiz also sent an urgent message to General Herron saying that he could not protect the American consulate.[95] In response, Herron put three regiments under arms, sent forty men of the 20th Wisconsin Infantry to seize the ferry, and dispatched four companies of the same regiment under Col. Henry Bertram, along with a battery of the 1st Missouri Artillery, across the river to rescue Pierce.[96] Herron also sent notes to both Ruiz and Cortina explaining that the Federals were crossing into Mexico only to protect the American consulate and would "take no part in the fight."[97] Colonel Bertram, in the midst of the fighting, arrived at the American consulate to find not only Pierce, but the British consul and representatives from both Ruiz and Cortina demanding to know what American soldiers were doing on Mexican soil.[98]

A dapper Cortina poses in Matamoros about the time he became governor of Tamaulipas. (Institute of Texan Cultures at San Antonio)

During the night, Cortina gained ground, but Ruiz still held the plaza and could hold out until morning when wagons would arrive to evacuate the consulate, Colonel Bertram wrote.[99] During the heaviest of the fighting, lawless bands, some attached to neither Ruiz nor Cortina, looted and plundered.

With daylight creeping into the narrow streets, Cortina's men continued to fight their way, house by house, street by street, until they had gained the plaza. Realizing the tide of battle had shifted, the forces of Ruiz, low on ammunition and demoralized, began to fall back and eventually flee; Cortina's cavalry was said to have "dashed through the streets striking down the fleeing fugitive[s]."[100] By noon, Cortina had successfully routed Ruiz and was in complete control of the town. Hundreds of Ruiz's men escaped by swimming the Rio Grande to Brownsville with most of his officers.[101] After eighteen hours of continuous carnage and bloodletting, the battle for Matamoros was over. As many as three hundred men were said to have died in the town, including all of Ruiz's artillerymen who fell at their guns; among the fallen was ex-governor Albino López, a prominent Ruiz partisan.[102] "We have lost everything," Ruiz told Pres. Benito Juárez.[103]

Within hours of the cessation of hostilities, Cortina proclaimed himself governor of Tamaulipas. In fewer than five years he had risen from a little-known and illiterate Cameron County ranchero to the pinnacle of power in Tamaulipas.

On 14 January, only one day after the fight with Ruiz, Cortina issued a pronunciamiento to the citizens of Matamoros, a copy of which can be found in the papers of Benito Juárez.[104]

* * * * * * * * * *

PRONUNCIAMIENTO

H. Matamoros

14 January 1864

The Citizen Colonel Juan N. Cortina, Chief of Forces of this Plaza, to its inhabitants:

Fellow Citizens:

You have been witnesses to the wavering politics that have upset this beautiful city since last November 7th and of the conduct I have observed until the treaties signed the 1st of this month.

I shall impose on you to permit me to tell you of the past occurrences and of the causes that obligated me to act in the way you saw.

Hopeful of avoiding further conflicts in this town, I ratified the aforementioned treaties in an effort to assure order and peace.

Unfortunately, our fellow citizen Gen. Manuel Ruiz, by his conduct, demonstrated his unwillingness to comply with such solemn pact, swearing allegiance only to gain control of the situation.

That civil servant, sadly remembered, began by demanding the ousting of forces guarding this plaza without provision for the necessary appeals, ignoring what is expressly prevented by the last member of the commission of treaties.

The 5th of the same basis, written suspiciously, was also violated by Ruiz, that Mr. Serna will face no responsibility for his public actions is the same thing to honor his obligation, when orders expedited against customs for payment of the loan contracted under commerce by Gov. Jesús de la Serna, were refused by that office.

These circumstances, in addition to the reiterated warnings of General Ruiz's hostilities towards me, forced me to prepare myself by neither falling prey to his ill will, nor exposing my comrades to the furor of such a vengeful enemy.

I have, therefore, placed myself on the defensive, but without taking any steps that may endanger public tranquility, and we have given witness to an act of outrageous barbarism: the horrible assassination of noted patriot commander Octaviano Cárdenas—cruelly and cowardly sacrificed, without justice or any of the requirements which the law provides, without even identifying him or executing him at the plaza or other public site, but rather, in a cell, in an inquisitorial style, only a few minutes after his apprehension.

A similar attempt against one of my better officials produced in me courage, an inexplicable effect within me once the victim was laid out and the monstrosity of the crime considered.

I restrained, however, those impulses that raged within me, in accordance with my resolution not to use arms; but Ruiz's forces opened fire upon my men, forcing me into combat, with fortune on my side. Those brave men accompanying me obtained a complete victory, with the enemies of peace hastily retreating.

In the midst of the bitterness that my soul suffered for the spilled blood of my fellow patriots in combat, I can't do anything less than congratulate myself and the inhabitants of this city, for the seed of discord has disappeared as the man hated by all social classes, exists no more.

Fellow Citizens:

I have complied with my duty of informing you of recent incidents and of the reasons for my conduct.

The leaderless nature of the state remains because of its lack of primary authorities, [and] has imposed upon me the obligation of resuming the political and military command, until the Supreme General Government, to whom I render account of occurrences, resolves otherwise in a most convenient manner.

In the short period after our victory, you have had occasion to observe my actions and those of the armed forces under my command.

Despite the unfavorable slurs against the citizen Ruiz, I have procured those acts which condemn such gratuitous imputations and place us in the category of civilized men—humane, generous, and lovers of social guarantees; because nothing could justly accuse us of having soiled our triumph with an act of cruelty; no one has been persecuted or molested, and the residents of Matamoros have been respected in their persons and interests.

My program, for the time being is to preserve peace. I promise in this solemn document observance of the law, effectiveness of individual guarantees, security of peace and union of Mexicans, and promotion of anything that will enhance the growth of our State.

To obtain these commendable objectives, I rely on the cooperation of my compatriots, with your patriotism and enlightenment. Forever those resentments borne from parted spirits and let us give to the world a testimony that we are worthy successors to the Hidalgos and Morelos.

Long live Mexico! Long live independence! Long live the State of Tamaulipas!

Juan N. Cortina

Cortina also rose to become a general in the army of Benito Juárez. (Institute of Texan Cultures at San Antonio)

5

After seizing power in Matamoros in November 1863, Cortina moved to establish communications with the wealthy, independent, and powerful caudillo of Nuevo León and Coahuila, the "Lion of the North,"—Santiago Vidaurri. Hearing that Cortina was in power, Vidaurri had written earlier asking Cortina for arms.[105] Fearful of being attacked by Ruiz, Cortina seemed reluctant to send the arms unless Vidaurri would send reinforcements from Monterrey.

At this critical time in Mexican history, events in northern Mexico were dramatically affected by the flight of Pres. Benito Juárez and the Republican government from the capital. After a siege of almost two months, the French Army under Gen. Elie Frédéric Forey had captured Puebla on 16 May 1863, and less than a month later had triumphantly entered Mexico City.[106] By December, Gen. Tomás Mejía had driven Juárez and his liberal army from San Luis Potosí and it appeared that both Tampico and Matamoros would fall. Nothing could stop the French, it seemed. In Monterrey, Vidaurri began to sway in the wind. To assure his allegiance, Juárez made him military *comandante* of Tamaulipas. But by the time Juárez arrived in Saltillo in January 1864, just as Cortina and Ruiz were dueling for control of Matamoros, Vidaurri continued to vacillate. He remained fearful that Juárez would demand the customs receipts from Piedras Negras, opposite Eagle Pass, where Texas cotton diverted from the lower Rio Grande Valley was helping to produce revenues of $40,000 to $50,000 each month.[107]

As Juárez entered Saltillo with his small army, Cortina sent his brother, José María, to see the president. José María carried a badly needed $20,000 for the ever-dwindling Mexican Army, along with a letter from Cortina pledging his loyalty to the government.[108] Throughout February 1864, Cortina continued to correspond with Juárez, always assuring the president of his loyalty and promising to send more money. On 6 February, he sent an additional $25,000 to Juárez with assurances of more as soon as the customs houses at Mier and Nuevo Laredo could be secured.[109] Three weeks later, Cortina forwarded Juárez $40,000.[110] But later in February, alarming news arrived in Matamoros from Monterrey. Vidaurri had pronounced against Juárez.

Although Vidaurri had warned him to stay away, Juárez entered Monterrey on 12 February 1864 with one thousand three hundred men. Vidaurri was nowhere to be seen, having barricaded himself in the Ciudadela, a fortress within the city. On the following day, Juárez finally found Vidaurri, and in a heated exchange, Vidaurri's son drew a pistol and threatened Juárez.[111] As the beleaguered little president fled through the streets in his carriage with Vidaurri's soldiers in pursuit, Vidaurri declared himself in open revolt. Reaching Saltillo, Juárez struck back by issuing a decree separating Coahuila from Nuevo León and declaring Nuevo León in open rebellion.

At this moment, Cortina, too, could have wavered. More importantly, the loss of Tamaulipas may well have doomed Juárez, for although he would later abandon the liberal cause, Cortina's loyalty to Juárez and the republic at this time in Mexican history, as expressed in his 27 February 1864 pronunciamiento to his soldiers, was a crowning moment in his military career.

In Monterrey, Vidaurri, fearful that Juárez would return with a large army, fled with his treasury north for the border. Halfway between the Nuevo León capital and the border, on a plain near the foothills of the Sierra Madre at Villa Aldama, Vidaurri's army was overtaken and crushed by the liberals.[112] As many of the defeated *norteños* now swore allegiance to Juárez, Vidaurri raced on to the Rio Grande to find safety in Laredo, Texas, under the protection of Col. Santos Benavides, a loyal Confederate and long-time friend.[113]

By early April, Juárez had set up his government in Monterrey but was forced to flee when the French marched on the city in August. Fleeing the advancing French Army, Juárez simply disappeared into the arid wastes of northern Mexico, later to appear at El Paso del Norte, a community on the Rio Grande that would change its name in 1888 to honor the liberal leader. At this point the cause of the Mexican liberals appeared to be on the ropes. With the governors of Chihuahua and Sonora wavering as Vidaurri had done, the liberal cause seemed all but dead. As Ferdinand Maximilian Joseph and Marie Charlotte Amélie Léopoldine arrived to assume the throne in Mexico City, Juan N. Cortina, governor of Tamaulipas, braced for the arrival of the French Army in Tamaulipas.

* * * * * * * * * *

PRONUNCIAMIENTO

Heroic Matamoros

27 February 1864

THE CITIZEN COL. JUAN N. CORTINA, GOVERNOR AND MILI-
TARY COMMANDANT OF THE FREE AND SOVEREIGN STATE
OF TAMAULIPAS, TO THE TROOPS OF THIS GARRISON.

Companions-at-arms:

Inexplicable is the feeling that my heart has had in recognizing
the documents that inform us of the recent events that have
occurred in the capital of the State of Nuevo León. When the
invader, thanks to our domestic fights that weakened us and not
due to their courage, have occupied some important plazas of the
interior, believes himself dominating the country and affects not
to exist in another government but on the one emanating from
the will of their bayonets, the Supreme Constitutional
Government resolved to transfer its residency to Monterrey and
there, where it only expected demonstrations of respect and
adhesion that would be an insult to the invaders, its authority is
contested, conditions for its residency have been set, and finally,
the Governor of the State himself who was supposed to be the
first to show his patriotism and abnegation, threatens it, and
trying to provoke a conflict, prepares himself to resist with arms
the force that escorted the Supreme leader of the Nation, who full
of prudence since other times has proved with greatness that he
knows how to face death, returns again to Saltillo, obvious of evils
of incalculable transcendence.

Whatever the motives that forced the citizen Santiago Vidaurri
to give this step, they had to, as it has been done by other states to
postpone it for better times. Today the question is to be or not to
be and in vain we will strive to sustain such or what ever formula,
if the existence of the soil in which it must take place, is answered
by an invader whom thanks to these disturbances advances with
slow but sure step to their possession and destruction of the exis-
tent.

The acts, for the same consummated in Nuevo León, with diminution to the National dignity outraged in its legitimate representative, are highly immoral and attemptive; they have discover, if are not remedied by its author, and incredible bottom of ambition and thirst for command and it is like that, as it has now been understood, this government tries to abrogate faculties that only reside in the supreme authority and handing its hands toward Tamaulipas, believes to be able to erect in it a Government that will help him in their attemptive objectives.

This will not be. God lives! While one of the combatants of the 12th and 13th of January breathes, no intruder will be mixed in our politics. Tamaulipas, jealous of the national good and its own, is ready to defend its immunity and its current government, resolved to severely and energetically punish those who in moments in which the national makes its last efforts to save motive that is invoked it not enough to cover the crime of treason to the motherland and the state.

You have to be vigilant, soldiers of the Republic and Liberty; that the invaders and traitors may find you with arms ready and the match lighted; you are defending the immunities of the National Government, Independence of the motherland, and the pride and dignity of the always free state of Tamaulipas.

Let us prove to the world that there is no danger that will make a Tamaulipas solider turn back and that, always loyal and coura- geous, your scream of war should be: Long live the Supreme Constitutional Government! Long live Independence! Long live the State of Tamaulipas!

Juan N. Cortina

6

Cortina's 1870 biography was penned by "Various Citizens of Tamaulipas" in response to the publication in Mexico City of Count Emile de Kératry's *Rise and Fall of the Emperor Maximilian.* Kératry, a prolific writer, had served in the French Contra Guerrillas under the dreaded cigar-chewing Col. Charles Dupin during the period of the intervention.[114] Five editions of his books were published in Europe with the French and English editions being circulated in Mexico and the United States.[115]

Kératry was critical of Maximilian for attempting to deal with Cortina, saying that the emperor had been "ignorant to pardon Cortina."[116] Specifically, Kératry quoted a May 1865 letter from Marshal Achille Francois Bazaine to Maximilian in which the marshal warned the Austrian emperor that "the odious part taken by the latter [Cortina] renders him for ever unworthy of your majesty's clemency."[117] Kératry, who was an aide-de-camp of Bazaine, concluded that Cortina was little more than an "irregular general . . . a thief, as cowardly as he was unruly" and "notorious for his treachery."[118]

Angered, Cortina fired back through the "Various Citizens of Tamaulipas" that he had been "rudely attacked," and demanded that Kératry's work not be "classed as historical truth."[119] To Cortina, it was necessary to set the record straight. In particular, Cortina objected to statements by Kératry that when he had realigned himself with the liberals, he had plotted "to deliver the port of Matamoros to [Miguel] Negrete . . . by virtue of a heavy sum of money."[120]

In the most part, the biography is an explanation of Cortina's decision to support the Empire, claiming that his objective was to save his army and salvage his artillery. Much of what the "Various Citizens of Tamaulipas" have to say is true, although Cortina's motives in supporting the Imperialists at such a crucial time on the border are difficult to judge.

The biography includes a brief mention of Cortina's role in the Mexican War, when, after the battles of Palo Alto and Resaca de la Palma, he was forced to flee into the deserts of northern Mexico. The biography also includes Cortina's version of the shooting of Marshal Robert Shears in Brownsville's Market Square in July 1859; also of note is his account of the early support he gave Gen. Ignacio Comonfort against the French in 1862-63. Although he was not at Puebla on historic Cinco de Mayo 1862, Cortina makes it clear he was with Ignacio Comonfort in an attempt to relieve the starving city during the lengthy French siege the following year.

The citizen-authors also struggle to explain Cortina's reasons for executing José María Cobos and Rómulo Vila in Matamoros in January 1864—an event that apparently played heavily on Cortina's mind. The biography furthermore attempts to rationalize the caudillo's reasons for turning against Gov. Manuel Ruiz.

The short study was first published as a pamphlet in Mexico City in July 1870.[121] It is obvious the "Citizens of Tamaulipas," although quite knowledgeable of ancient history and mythology, obtained their information from the wily caudillo himself, though the date given for Cortina's birth is questionable.

The pamphlet may have been translated by veteran border journalist Henry Alonso Maltby, owner and editor of the Brownsville *Daily Ranchero*.[122] Maltby ran the "interesting" biography in four issues of the *Daily Ranchero* in 1870. No copies of the Spanish version are known to exist; consequently, a comparison with what appeared in the *Daily Ranchero* is not possible. Slightly edited, the *Ranchero* version follows.

* * * * * * * * * *

BIOGRAPHY

July 1870

Juan Nepomuceno Cortina

Juan N. Cortina was born in Camargo in the month of March 1824.* His parents were Trinidad Cortina and María Estéfana Goseascochea. There he spent a few years of his childhood, until his parents moved to Matamoros where they had their interest. The bandit, the adventurer described by [Emile] Kératry, was the son of property holders and said property is still in possession of the family.

In the years 1845-46, the unhappy war between Mexico and the United States began. The latter did not understand yet that nothing weakens great nations more than extension of territory. And the eagerness of the neighboring republic to extend its limit, favored the annexionists and their troops, and invaded Mexican soil.

Then the frontier states of our country raised the first cry of war, and their sons hastened to the conflict. Cortina then enlisted in a squadron organized in Matamoros, as a private soldier. It was not ambition which moved him to take up arms, because notwithstanding the comforts which he enjoyed, he took up a gun to fight against the invaders.

Kératry, the French historian, asserts that Cortina was an improvised general; in this he is not correct, as it always happens when one writes of a country without studying it and without having a correct judgment of its prominent men. Cortina rose slowly through all the grades of the military. His officers, seeing the calmness and valor of Cortina, made him a second sergeant, charging him with dangerous duties, and sending him constantly to scout near the enemy. Since then, he is being accompanied by his faithful friend, the valiant Col. Arocha, who has rendered his services to the country since he was a private soldier.

---

*Cortina's birth is generally given as 16 May 1824. A Camargo baptismal record has not been located.

But Cortina not only offered to the country his blood, but he also contributed to the war expenses with his own interests, until they were nearly exhausted. The rest of them fell into possession of the enemy when the troops had to retire giving up their ground before the superior numbers of the invaders.

Then began a life of proscription for Cortina. During three years, he had to wander about, either fighting detailed detachments of Americans or fleeing in the deserts, until peace was restored by the treaty of Guadalupe, the invaders evacuating Mexican soil in a definite manner in 1848. Cortina then retired to private life, devoting himself to replace his interests which had suffered so much.

But his lands, the only property which he had left, were situated in that part of the territory, which after the treaty was given up to the United States. And it was a repugnance to his patriotism to be obliged to live among the enemies whom he hated so much. These sentiments, in a spirit of Cortina's temper, could not help from breaking out into a rage later.

In fact, exasperated on seeing the treatment to which the Mexicans were subjected by the Americans, one day he raised the first cry of insurrection in the streets of Brownsville. A sheriff arrested a Mexican and struck him several blows. Cortina spoke on his behalf and received insults as the only reply. A fight ensued in which the sheriff was killed.* American forces came to his aid, and Cortina, on horseback and alone, fell back to the Rastro, where he was met by some Mexicans who joined him. With them he drove back the American detachment, pursuing them to the streets of Brownsville and killing many.

Since then Cortina returned to that hazardous and fighting life in the midst of the American territory, proclaimed an outlaw pursued like a wild beast, but inspiring terror among the Yankees. It was the last vivid protest of the Mexicans against that iniquitous usurpation.

---

*Marshall Robert Shears was wounded in the shoulder. See the introduction to Pronunciamiento 1.

At the last persecution Cortina came very near being captured; the Americans found traitors who joined them, and making it easier for them to apprehend Cortina because their allies knew the country perfectly, as that cunning and surprising warrior. The Mexican soldier at last had to cross the frontier. But a following incident justified the war without quarter which he made on the Americans of Brownsville. These adventurers disowned the government of the United States, and the latter had to pursue them actively to subject them, and suppress their depredations. The Mexican population of Texas had reason then not to tolerate the yoke nor the outrages of these disorganized bands, and Cortina had an ample right to take up arms to obtain the guarantees which neither the Mexican government claimed, nor the American government caused to be respected; guarantees which the Treaty of Guadalupe-Hidalgo granted to the Mexican population of the ceded territory.

Afterwards followed that internal strife which rendered the frontier states, as much by local questions, as when the echo of the revolution sounded, which in different phases, shook the republic, in the contest inaugurated by the liberal party against the retrograde men. It would be a long task to mention those events, but it suffices to say that Cortina figured in them always on the side of the liberal party; Kératry is unjust in accusing him for his defections; he never will be able to justify them.

The sad moments for the republic arrived. The church party wearied of losing on every ground, and feeling its death approaching, resorted to the last extreme, to treason, and drew foreign troops to their country to impose a retrograde government.

The three allied nations arrived on the waters of Veracruz, and, without previous declaration of war, occupied the city, and advanced by the tierra caliente. Mexico shuddered, feeling its nationality outraged, and fought on every ground.

A conference took place at Soledad, and there, [Manuel] Doblado, Mexican minister, matched the European diplomats, obliging [Dubois de] Saligny to resign his office, to lie and to fill himself with mire; soiling at the same time the flag which he represented.*

The treaties of Soledad being null, the English and Spanish forces reembarked; France was obliged to fall back on her word, and the time arrived when only the voice of the cannon was heard.

Mexico was not prepared for the strife, but the patriotism supplied all, and the 5th of May marked the prologue of that immortal episode, which was called the war of our second independence.

The French who had advanced on Puebla were obliged to fall back on Orizaba; several months elapsed, during which time both sides prepared for the conflict.

The invaders were reinforced; Mexico suffered reverses at [Cerro] Borrego and Barranca Seca, and, finally, the seize of Puebla took place.

The most distant states had sent their contingent of men; the country was determined to fight until death, and her sons hastened to group around the flag of [Ignacio] Zaragoza.**

Meanwhile a noted and really grand incident was taking place on the frontier; let us give a brief account.

[Ignacio] Comonfort, from his place of banishment, had heard the voice of his country; and that great heart offered it its sword in

---

*At La Soledad, a village near Orizaba, on 19 February 1862, Gen. Juan Prim, commanding the Spanish expedition to Mexico, and Manuel Doblado, Mexican Foreign Minister, agreed that the allied expeditionary force could advance into the highlands while negotiations over the European claims would begin at Orizaba. Dubois de Saligny, a leading exponent of intervention, had become the French minister to Mexico in 1860. Doblado, who had previously served as military governor of Jalisco, later accompanied Juárez to Saltillo, Monterrey, and El Paso del Norte (present-day Ciudad Juárez). He died in New York City in 1865.

**Born in Goliad, Texas, the bespectacled Zaragosa became the popular hero of Cinco de Mayo for his gallant defense of Puebla in 1862, only to die five months later of typhoid fever.

the simple character of a soldier.* But he had committed the crime of coup d'etat, and the Republican Party, susceptible and suspicious, feared that the ex-president would come inspired by personal ambition, his presence in Mexico being, during that period, a new cause for dissension, and food for the civil strife destroying us. But the voice of self-sacrifice, everywhere makes itself heard. Comonfort was accepted by the government of the republic, which charged him to bring to the capital the northern contingents. [Santiago] Vidaurri, still faithful to his country, was the first one who dared to receive the exile, and afforded him all the means of his power.**

Cortina at the head of a squadron, perfectly organized, armed and mounted, joined Gen. Comonfort; he received from the headquarters a major's commission, and his squadron received the title, which it bears up to this day, "Frontier Scouts."

Cortina marched with his forces to the siege of Puebla, and formed a part of the army of the center. And thus he took a part in the battle of San Lorenzo, which turned the fortune in favor of the heroic City of Zaragoza.***

The government abandoned the capital and went to San Luis; the army also retired. Cortina had now rose to the rank of Lieutenant-Colonel, conferred upon him by the executive as a reward for his important services to the national cause.

Cortina appeared before the government at San Luis, and the latter ordered him to Matamoros to organize his forces. In fact, he increased his squadron to three hundred men, all his soldiers being volunteers.

---

*Thrust into the presidency in 1855 and caught between the liberals and conservatives, Comonfort resigned in 1858 and fled to the United States. In 1862, he returned to Mexico, raised an army in support of the republic, and became secretary of war. He was ambushed and killed by imperialists at Molino de Soria near Guanajuato on 14 November 1863.

**Santiago Vidaurri was the powerful caudillo of Nuevo León and Coahuila. See the introduction to Pronunciamiento 5.

***In an attempt to relieve the starving and besieged garrison at Puebla, Comonfort lost one thousand men, killed and wounded, and another thousand as prisoners at San Lorenzo, ten miles outside Puebla on 7 May 1863.

Here we are going to relate a most terrible incident; we have to touch a very important event, on account of the fatal results which might have attended the national cause; we will mention it as briefly as possible.

Demoralization had extended all over the republic; the defection of many was announced already, and the traitors unblushingly labored in favor of intervention. The agents of the conservative party were all over the country, either propagating imperial doctrines or preparing the elements to adhere to the French plan. This caused a disturbance in the states, and the authorities governing in virtue of a state of siege, without any law to guide them, were in open conflict against the people.

The situation of Matamoros was typical of this general disturbance. The government of the state, Don Manuel Ruiz, was on the brink of a volcano, because the excitement of the people, made his administration unable to evade the crisis.

At this critical moment José [María] Cobos, the active church party chieftain, arrived at the head of a force of adventurers, sent by his party to see if they could succeed in taking possession of the port. He depended on powerful aid in the city, and no doubt but that Gov. Ruiz was lost.*

Cortina, with his profound instinct, foresaw the danger, and anticipated it to Ruiz, leaving the city for a neighboring country house.

In fact, Cobos entered the city, aided by some, imprisoned Ruiz and his employees, and obeyed by the troops, he held a meeting of notables and issued his act of adherence to the intervention.

Cortina, meanwhile, arriving suddenly, visited the quarters, harangued the troops, and captivated the loyalty of the officers, who pledged their word not to obey any orders but his own; he held a conference with the Liberals, and went to the palace where Cobos was at work on his plan against the independence of the nation.

---

*See the introduction to Pronunciamiento 3.

As soon as Cobos heard of the arrival of Cortina he sent for him and informed him of the plan. Cortina quietly heard it read, after the conclusion of which he asked for it, folded it, and coolly put it in his pocket. He told Cobos that it did not suit him and went down to the yard where his troops were. He sent an officer with a small guard of soldiers to arrest Cobos and [Rómulo] Vila, his secretary, taking them to where the troops were. It was thus made, and the two revolutionists were taken to the lagoon and shot.

The frontier was saved.

After the execution, Cortina returned to the palace, he liberated the governor, and informed him of what had taken place; Ruiz then ordered the bodies to be identified. The conspirators were eclipsed, and no one thought any more about their betraying their country.

Gen. Ruiz continued exercising his functions as Governor.

But notwithstanding a kind of antagonism existed between the Governor of the State and Cortina. This phenomenon occurred frequently in the cities which still remained faithful to the republic, and can easily be explained. The civil authorities wanted to govern in those critical moments, making use of the usual means whilst the military leaders had a conviction which was the result of extraordinary and energetic measures a barrier could he put to treason and to the foreigners invading the autonomy of the nation. And the military officers were right, because the stoutest hearts had become demoralized, when the foreboding of defeat was general among all Mexicans, it would have been impossible to obtain a single recruit to increase the number of troops, or a single dollar to sustain them.

Be it as it may, Gen. Ruiz abandoned the city of Matamoros and went to San Luis, where he appeared before the government, making such a picture of the situation of Matamoros as judged by his prejudiced spirit.

The government at the same time fearing a retreat, hastened to give troops to the governor so as to preserve order in Matamoros.

As soon as he arrived in that city, Cortina placed himself at his orders.

Then followed events which we would like to blot from the history of our country; let us narrate them rapidly.

The antagonism which existed before hand among the two entities there facing each other, became more excited instead of calming with the presence of the Federal troops; the provincialism, the jealousy of the people against each other, and a thousand other causes of this kind excited it.

The situation became worse every day, until one day, [Octaviano] Cárdenas, one of Cortina's most valiant officers, was arrested and taken to one of the quarters of Ruiz's troops and there shot.

We have to advert that the center of the city was occupied by Ruiz's troops and the outskirts was occupied by Cortina with his men, a dividing line existed between them, which helped to avoid encounters which might disturb public order and terminate in a revolution.

As soon as the news of Cárdenas' execution became known the volcano erupted. Cortina and his men attacked the place, defeated the troops of Ruiz and occupied the entire city, notwithstanding their inferior numbers.

Who was responsible for these events? History and the intimate conscience of each one of the personages who figured in that sorrowful drama will answer better than us, who only limit ourselves to the truth.

But we ought to remark here that after this incident the Supreme Government promoted Cortina to the rank of colonel, appointing him governor and military commander of the state of Tamaulipas. This meant that the cabinet of Juárez knew how to appeal to the local exigencies of the people, or that it understood that the services which Cortina and his men would render to the national cause were not to be scorned.

During the administration of Cortina, a phenomenon took place, which if it had been known by Kératry he would not have written in his book, what he wrote about the governor of Matamoros.

The adventurer, the bandit described by Kératry, did all he could for the welfare of the people, notwithstanding the state of siege and the general situation of the republic. He organized troops, and as soon as he learned that Vidaurri had proclaimed against the Supreme Government he sent them to aid the latter, this event "denies" the statement of Kératry, because he states that the general was loyal, inasmuch as that would have been the best occasion to revolt if he had wished to do so.

But this was not all. Kératry assures us that the towns suffered the exactions of Cortina. The bandit as he calls him, delivered to the Supreme Government one hundred and forty-five thousand dollars in three parts, the first of which amounted to sixty thousand dollars, and was carried to the President by Cortina's brother; the second one amounting to twenty-five thousand dollars was delivered to [Justo] Benítez, at the present chief clerk in the war office and the last one of sixty thousand dollars was received by Mr. [José María] Iglesias, actually Minister of Justice, during his visit to Matamoros.* These facts speak for themselves.

The Supreme Government knew how to appreciate such important services by rendering a homage or appreciation to Cortina for his conduct, giving his troops important duties to perform, and ordering that the battalion organized by the General's brother should be called "Battalion Cortina."

In Matamoros, Camargo and other towns in that state, still exist some material improvements made during Cortina's short administration.

---

*Benítez was a young lawyer friend of Juárez. Along with Gen. Porfirio Díaz, he was captured by the French, but was able to escape and rejoin the liberals. He later became secretary of the treasury under Díaz. Appointed minister of justice in 1863, Iglesias went on to become minister of government in 1868. After the death of Juárez, he attempted unsuccessfully to topple Pres. Sebastián Lerdo de Tejada from power. He later challenged Díaz for power but went into exile in 1877.

Meanwhile the French invasion was advancing powerfully to the frontier. The Imperial forces of [Tomás] Mejía were approaching rapidly, while a French column was marching parallel with them in the direction of Tampico, under the command of [Charles] Dupin, of such sorrowful remembrance.*

Before such military operations of an enemy so numerous and well organized, Cortina understood the difficultness of the situation. The government had retired to Chihuahua, the national forces were retreating at the same time, while others dispersed or disbanded; the hour for the conflict had arrived.

General Cortina found himself shut up in a circle of bayonets. He could not communicate with his government, neither could he hope for aid. He then thought about saving his armaments, the artillery and the abundant war material in the city.

With that object he addressed the nearest American officer, proposing to him to allow the war material to be crossed to the other side of the river, and thus save this property belonging to the Mexican nation, by depositing it in the warehouses of the United States, inasmuch as the most friendly relation and harmony existed between the two countries.

The American officer was perfectly willing, but he informed General Cortina that Brownsville was occupied by Confederate troops, and this being the place by which the material should be crossed, it would have been inevitably lost.

Then there was no hope, then, of realizing that plan.

---

*In command of the French Contra Guerillas, Colonel Dupin was a veteran of the Crimean War and colonial conflicts in China and Algeria. In 1864, after the pacification of Vera Cruz, he was sent to northeastern Mexico where he quickly gained a reputation for ruthlessness. See the introduction to Pronunciamiento 7. Mejía, an Indian cacique from Querétaro, had supported the conservatives in the War of the Reform and became a leading general under the French during the period of the Empire. Appointed military commander of Tamaulipas, he occupied Matamoros in September 1864, but evacuated the city following the defeat of Gen. Pierre Jean Joseph Jeanningros' army at Santa Gertrudis near Camargo. Although he was offered his freedom at Querétaro, the always-chivalrous Mejía refused and was executed along with Maximilian and Miguel Miramón on the Cerro las Campanas on 19 June 1867.

On the day following the conference with the American officer, General Cortina received a commissioner from Mejía, the imperial officer, who informed him that he was at Charco Escondido, twenty-five leagues from Matamoros, with his whole division. The commissioner besides requested that a conference should be held between both officers, suggested the next day, if Cortina accepted.

Cortina agreed, and designated Santa Rosalía, telling the commissioner that he would advance on the road until he met the vanguard of the Imperial troops, so that the officer in command should advise Mejía.

In those critical moments General Aureliano Rivera arrived in the city offering his services to General Cortina; the latter accepted them quickly and called together all the officers of the garrison. When they were all present he explained to them the situation of the city with the enemy's approach; but that he was determined to defend it to the last. He introduced them to General Rivera and advised them to place themselves at his orders.

Col. Servando Canales opposed that measure stating that it would be impossible to defend the city with such small numbers against the superior army of the enemy which was advancing rapidly.* And besides, he refused to be under the orders of anyone.

Cortina then understood that all was lost, inasmuch as demoralization and dissension existed among the troops in the city.

At that moment a scout informed him that the officer in command of the vanguard at Santa Rosalía was falling back before the enemy's forces.

Immediately the counsel broke up, and Cortina ordered his troops to be in readiness to go out. He was about to do so when

---

*The son of Antonio Canales, Servando Canales fought against the United States in 1846-47 and the liberals in the War of the Reform. Born in Camargo, Canales became a general under Juárez. He served five times as governor of Tamaulipas (1866, 1870, 1872, and 1876) and was a political rival of Cortina. See introduction to Pronunciamiento 10.

he was informed that Colonel Canales with the 7th Battalion of Tamaulipas, under his command, had crossed the river, delivering his armament to the Confederate troops.

The garrison had now lost by this some of its best troops, and was now reduced to only three hundred men of the "Frontier Scouts." In view of such sad news, Cortina's spirit failed him and he went out to meet Mejía. The conference took place on the following day.

Mejía, the Imperial General, stated to Cortina that with the number of troops and the war material he had he would attack him without fail, and that to avoid the shedding of useless blood ordered him to surrender the city with all his troops.

Cortina scorned that preposition, saying that he preferred death rather than to accept an agreement that would stain his good name, and fail in his duty as a soldier of the republic.

The discussion between them became more and more interesting, until at last it was agreed that Cortina should remain under Mejía's orders with all the troops under his command and the war material he possessed. But it was stipulated that he would not recognize the Empire, neither would he sign the act of adherence, that the French should not occupy the state of Tamaulipas and they should retire to the Sierra. Mejía having accepted this proposition, he occupied the city of Matamoros.

Let us analyze cautiously this action of Cortina, subjecting it to the most severe criticism, inasmuch as it has been the one from which Kératry has criticized him the most, and has been the cause for his writing of this biographical work. Let us blot out that shadow of treason thrown upon one of the Generals who has rendered most important services to the nation.

Cortina did not betray, but remained in a state of armed neutrality, caused by circumstances. Cortina subjected himself to Mejía because he could do no other. Since he found himself in that anonymous situation, three roads remained for him to take: fight and defend the city until death, cross the river, or subject himself as he did, obtaining greater advantages for his cause as we will explain hereafter. Let us examine each one of these cases.

To fight with three hundred men against five thousand besieging him was to shed blood in vain, to endanger the city, the families residing there, and the great many interests therein stored and all this without any probability of success, neither being aided, nor even having communication with the national government, which was at a considerable distance. Besides, in case Cortina was defeated he would lose all his material and armaments, which would later be of great usefulness to his country. And then it would not have been said that he met an honorable death. All the laws of war advised him to make agreements and he had not done so; his heroic stubbornness would have been subjected to a military trial. Besides, we ought to bear in mind the effervescence existing in the city, the evil disposition of the people, and that the retreat of Canales had left him without any support. For that reason, Gen. Cortina gave up the idea of sustaining a siege in that city which was not fortified, ammunitioned and sufficiently prepared, and the circuit of which could not have been covered by the small number of cavalry which remained faithful to him. To attempt such a thing was impossible.

He did not want to cross the river either, because that would have been delivering the material of war to the Confederates, which was to the nation equal to losing them, and he might have been held responsible for them.

He had to submit to the circumstances and place himself in a position of armed neutrality, in which he made the imperial officer by means of cunningness and energy.

This saved his troops, his material, and served for the liberal party which remained faithful in the traditions of independence, to have in them always a support.

Here is the charge of treason imputed upon him entirely vanished.

General Cortina, after the occupation of the city, went to the towns situated on the lower Río Bravo. The situation of Cortina was hazardous and difficult because he had to follow patiently the plan which he had proposed, and that was to remain near to the enemy until the occasion presented itself to enter anew the active services in favor of the national cause.

From this it will be seen that he proposed to avoid every encounter with the Liberal troops, and this explains why he avoided always meeting Canales, who had returned with forces to the Mexican side. Here is the reason for those irregular marches of Cortina from Camargo to Laredo and Mier, taking always an opposite direction to the place where Canales was.

But one day it was impossible to evade it; Canales was determined to fight and he attacked Cortina at Guerrero, and the latter being obliged to set in self-defense, defeated Canales. The aggressor was to blame and only ought to be regretted the brave officers who fell in this fight.

After that painful victory, Cortina returned to Mier, determined to take a definite part in clearing up that doubtful situation. He believed that the moment had arrived for him to prove by his acts that he had not been unfaithful to his country.

At Mier he received a letter from Colonel Gorrustieta, inviting him to hold a conference with General [Mariano] Escobedo at Davis [Rio Grande City].* Cortina willingly accepted the situation and went to Camargo.

Under his protection came Escobedo and Gorrustieta over to that city, and remained in accord with Cortina. The latter told them to use the funds of the Mier and New Laredo custom-houses, to organize troops, leaving his brother José María in Camargo to act in accord with them.

Cortina returned to Matamoros leaving a part of his brigade at San Fernando. There he received orders from Mejía to join

---

*Leading the liberal forces in Tamaulipas, Gen. Mariano Escobedo entered Matamoros in June of 1866 following the battle of Santa Gertrudis. He commanded the liberal army at Querétaro in 1867 and was appointed minister of war in 1876, only to be later exiled by Porfirio Díaz.

Larrumbide and pursue General [José María Jesús] Carbajal.* In fact, Cortina left for Padilla, and there he received an express from Carbajal asking him for information regarding the position of the traitors. Cortina pointed them out to him; telling him at the same time, if he was threatened by Larrumbide and Dupin to fall back on San Fernando where his troops were, and they would protect him.

It was at the beginning of the year 1865 when Cortina declared himself an open enemy to the Empire; he issued circulars to the people calling on them to report his movements; he captured one hundred infantry from Larrumbide, and ordered Colonel [José María] Cortina, his brother, to organize troops as fast as possible.

On the night of Holy Thursday, Cortina at the head of only fifty horsemen, fell upon the city of Matamoros, and caused the forces of Mejía to retire to the interior of the city. Pando, an Imperial officer, was killed in this affair.

By this audacious act, Cortina wished to test the public feeling, which he found in a favorable state, and took arms and ammunition out of Matamoros.

He had intentions to continue operating against the city, when his brave companion and friend, Don Esteban de la Garza, arrived, bringing the sad news that Colonel Cortina, his brother, had been imprisoned by Francisco de León, acting governor, Carbajal being absent. He left for Camargo immediately; on the road he found his brother who had escaped; but Cortina continued his march to that city to save his troops. There he received a courier from General [Miguel] Negrete, ordering him to operate against the enemy, until the Liberal troops arrived to besiege Matamoros.**

---

*Born in San Antonio and educated in Kentucky, Carbajal was the son-in-law of Martín de León and a relative of Cortina. He was active in the federalist cause along the Rio Grande in 1839-40, commanded a division in the Mexican Army in 1847, and led filibusters in the Merchants War. In 1862 he joined the liberal army and rose to become governor of Tamaulipas in September 1864 and again in March 1866, both times succeeding Cortina.

**A liberal general and hero of Cinco de Mayo, Negrete became minister of war in the Juárez government but pronounced against the republic at Puebla in 1869. Arrested, he was sentenced to death but was pardoned.

Cortina immediately undertook his march, and sent his brother, and his cousin, Garza, as commissioners to the General-in-Chief. These two gentlemen fulfilled their mission well, and Garza returned to General Cortina with some papers and instructions.

Since Negrete established his headquarters at Santa Rosalía, he sent for Cortina, ordering him to guide the movements of the army, as he had a good knowledge of the ground.

At last the siege commenced when suddenly it was broken up by Negrete, who retreated with the whole army to Monterrey, confiding in Cortina to cover that inexplicable retreat. Cortina did so while operating against the enemy, harassing them constantly.

After that, Escobedo besieged Matamoros, depending previously on General Cortina, who gave him important service on the day of the assault with him troops attacked the most important point and one of his battalions ended there.

The siege was also broken up, and Escobedo, as he retired, appointed Cortina General-in-Chief of the army around Matamoros.

It would be a long task to narrate each one of the engagements fought by Cortina. He was always in front of the enemy, either surprising him, or interrupting his communications; he cooperated the most in the destruction of the Empire.

Since then Cortina was in front of the enemy, capturing from him troops, wagons, and money. He was always tireless and determined to fight for the national cause.

At last Escobedo returned with the troops making up the Northern army, and defeated the Imperial General [Rafael] Olivera at Santa Gertrudis capturing a convoy. Cortina did not take part in this battle, because he was at San Fernando organizing his troops.

After the victory at Santa Gertrudis, a movement on Matamoros was made. The said city had been occupied by Gen. Carbajal.

Since then Gen. Cortina joined the army of Puebla, taking part in the siege of Querétaro and the siege of the city of Mexico, in both of which he rendered important services.

At last the republic was restored, France withdrew her troops before the threats of the United States, and the Empire which only depended on the fictitious aid of foreign troops, died in a lake of blood.

The independence was saved. But even then the revolutionary traditions had not been forgotten. A few malcontents ignited the soil of Puebla and the revolution headed by Negrete appeared anew, powerful and threatening. Then the government called on the troops in which it had more confidence; for that reason Gen. Cortina was ordered to take part in that campaign, in which he fulfilled his undertaking admirably.

In the fall of 1868 Cortina desired to retire to private life, and to that effect he asked and obtained permission from the Supreme Government to return to Tamaulipas.

On the way he received a communication from the Minister of War, ordering him not to make use of his license, but to join Gen. Escobedo, a pronunciamiento having broken out in Tamaulipas.

Cortina, always faithful and obedient, made the campaign until it ended in the year 1870, by the agreement made by Gen. [Sostenes] Rocha.

Peace did not last long. Revolution appeared again more powerful in the state of San Luis Potosí, and Gen. Escobedo called Gen. Cortina who joined him at Dolores Hidalgo, after overcoming numberless obstacles.

Cortina from that moment took a part in all the engagements which were fought even to the terrible battle of Obejo, in which he conducted himself in an honorable manner and officially received the approval of the government.* Colonel María Menchaca, an old companion of Gen. Cortina, was wounded in that battle.

The revolution had hardly ended when Bravo appeared without any flag or political party [and began] depredating upon the towns and haciendas on the Interior road, almost within sight of the capital, and leaving in his path a track of tears and blood. He was pursued in vain; Bravo, with his outlaw band, made his movements so rapidly, that it seemed impossible to overtake him. But the government confided his persecution to Cortina, and the latter overtook him and defeated him completely.

Afterwards he returned to the Capital, where he was called by the Supreme Government.

We have slowly run over the general's life, calumniated by a foreign writer; we have described the events, without passion, having authentic documents before us and the accounts of irreproachable witnesses; our object was to [refute] the unjust attacks made upon some Mexican generals; the good name of the country was involved in it too.

Gen. Cortina, a true republican soldier, brave, modest and faithful, never has sought for fame; he believed that he owed to his country the contingent of his blood, and has not shrunk from danger, when he has seen his soil profaned by the invader's foot. There are very few spirits who reach such grade of indignation as Cortina's, when he sees the liberty and independence of Mexico, attacked by armed foreigners.

Gen. Cortina ought to be, then, quiet in his conscience for what he has done, and with the vindication of his countrymen.

City of Mexico, July, 1870

Various Citizens of Tamaulipas

---

*A rebellion against the Juárez government was crushed with heavy casualties at Lo de Obejo near San Luis Potosí on 22 February 1870.

7

In September 1864 Cortina found himself trapped in Matamoros as an Imperialist army under Gen. Tomás Mejía moved from Bagdad on the coast upriver toward the town. Unable to retreat into the interior, Cortina, who had only recently survived an assassination attempt by two Frenchmen, considered crossing his artillery and twelve hundred-man army to the north bank to join the Union forces who, despite the Confederate occupation of Brownsville, were holding the lower Texas coast. Some Cortinistas did cross the river and a few even saw action in the Union ranks, twelve of whom were captured by the Rebels under Col. John S. Ford. Most of Cortina's army, however, was forced upriver by the advancing French. At this critical juncture, Cortina made one of the most fateful decisions of his life—one that would damage his already tarnished reputation and haunt him for decades. On 22 September 1864, as General Mejía led his army into Matamoros, Cortina received a commission in the Imperialist army.[123] He would later argue that to save his army and his artillery he had no choice but to cooperate with General Mejía. For several months thereafter he would remain loosely attached to the French Army.

But at San Fernando, on the coastal plain some eighty-five miles south of Matamoros, on 1 April 1865, Cortina reasserted his loyalty to Pres. Benito Juárez.[124] Within two weeks he had marched his army to the very gates of Matamoros, had overrun the town's defenses, had killed an Imperialist colonel and several of his men, had retrieved some military supplies he had previously concealed in the town, had stolen some horses for his men, and, in typical Cortina fashion, had galloped out of town.[125] During much of 1865, he remained active in the area between Ciudad Victoria and Monterrey in what amounted to a vicious, no-holds-barred, guerrilla war with Col. Charles Dupin and the dreaded French Contra Guerrillas.[126]

Returning to the border, Cortina, again governor of Tamaulipas, hammered at the defenses of Matamoros for two months. It was not until a large convoy of two hundred carts, escorted by eighteen hundred soldiers (many of them Austrian), bound from Matamoros to Monterrey, was set upon at the Santa Gertrudis hills near Camargo on 16 June 1866, that Imperialist control of Matamoros began to crumble.[127] With only seven hundred of the eighteen hundred men escaping, Santa Gertrudis became the Waterloo for the Imperialists in Tamaulipas and northern Mexico. On 23 June 1866 Matamoros surrendered.[128]

With the collapse of the Imperialist army in northern Mexico and Napoleon III's decision to order the French out of Mexico, Maximilian's empire began to crack and crumble. When the last of the French sailed away in March of 1867, liberal generals closed in on the last remaining Imperialist strongholds. Just as Maximilian prepared to defend the clerical cause to the end, Cortina marched his army to Querétaro in order to join other liberal generals in a siege that would last for seventy-one days. Finally, on the night of 14 May 1867, as the liberals were led into the city by an Imperialist officer turned traitor, Maximilian and his generals surrendered. Cortina would later claim that it was he and Gen. Juan Corona who captured Maximilian.[129] After the emperor's death by fusillade a month later on the barren Cerro de las Campañas, Cortina remained in the liberal cause.

Although Juárez was able to pacify much of Mexico, large regions in the north remained under control of regional caudillos and defiant caciques. Tamaulipas, in particular, fell into chaos and a state of utter lawlessness. On 9 June 1870, a defiant Gen. Pedro Martínez occupied Matamoros, saying that he came to "wage war on the dictatorship of Don Benito Juárez."[130] Within days Cortina was writing from Mexico City that he would march within a week with his cavalry to the relief of the town. Urging citizens not to join the rebels, Cortina asked all "good sons of Tamaulipas" to rally to the defense of the supreme government.[131] Arriving on the Rio Grande, Cortina chased General Martínez out of Matamoros and marched triumphantly into the town in the third week of September 1870.

Joyously welcomed as governor of Tamaulipas, Cortina was at the peak of his power. Even the American press applauded a return to law and order and prayed that he would end the cattle rustling on the border.[132] In Matamoros on 19 September 1870, Cortina issued a short pronunciamiento promising to end the lawlessness. The pronunciamiento was published by Henry A. Maltby in the

22 September issue of the Brownsville *Daily Ranchero.*[133] A second copy survived when Thomas F. Wilson, United States consul in Matamoros, clipped the pronunciamiento and sent it to Secretary of State Hamilton Fish in Washington.[134]

* * * * * * * * * *

PRONUNCIAMIENTO

H. Matamoros

19 September 1870

Juan N. Cortina, brigadier-general of the national army, in command of the 1st Tamaulipas brigade, to the inhabitants of the Northern District.

Fellow-Citizens:

The supreme magistrate of the republic, honoring me excessively with its confidence, has entrusted me with the pacification of this important part of the frontier, with the forces which have been under my orders. With this object, in a few days, the military line from this city to the line of the state of Nuevo León will be established, and the bands of highwaymen and kidnappers will soon be exterminated, because they will be pursued without rest at every hour and in every place. Travelers and pacific residents of the towns, will always find in me the most firm protector of the guarantees and security which our constitution grants to their persons and property. For such noble purposes your co-operation is depended on by your fellow-citizen and friend.

Juan N. Cortina

The fatigue from too many battles and political struggles is evident in the face of Cortina in this photograph taken around 1872. Three years later, Pres. Sebastián Lerdo de Tejada had him arrested and sent to Mexico City. (Carlos Larralde)

8

By 1875, the French had been chased from Mexico and the Emperor Maximilian von Hapsburg was dead. The little Zapotec Indian Benito Juárez was dead, too, succeeded as president in 1872 by Sebastián Lerdo de Tejada. Although no longer governor of Tamaulipas, Cortina remained as president of the Matamoros ayuntamiento.

For several years he had been accused by American authorities of masterminding the theft of thousands of head of cattle in South Texas. In the collateral violence of the "Skinning War," some of Cortina's men raided as far north as Nuecestown near Corpus Christi.[135] In retaliation for such raids, Texas Rangers invaded Mexico, burned, plundered, and indiscriminately hanged Mexicans.[136] Border violence threatened to drag the two republics into war and both countries sent commissions of investigation to the region. Although the U.S. Commission amassed a mountain of incriminating evidence against Cortina, the Mexican Commission largely exonerated him.[137]

William Steele, Texas adjutant general, was convinced that Cortina was in control of a border army of no fewer than two thousand "armed adherents."[138] The powerful caudillo, Steele told Gov. Richard Coke, was "the recognized head and protector of all of the cattle thieves and murderers from Camargo to the mouth of the Rio Grande."[139] Cortina was even accused of shipping stolen Texas cattle from the mouth of the Rio Grande to Havana, Cuba. Brig. Gen. Edward Otho Cresap Ord, commanding the Department of Texas and the United States Army on the Rio Grande, agreed with Steele.

In Mexico City, John W. Foster, United States minister to Mexico, pressured J. M. Lafragua, Mexican minister of foreign affairs, to remove Cortina to some remote part of the Mexican republic. "His removal," Foster told Lafragua, "would have a very salutatory effect upon the frontier and be accepted as an act of conciliation and peace toward the United States."[140] When Lafragua replied that Cortina was mayor of Matamoros, a civil position not subject to the whims of the central government, Foster countered that Cortina still held a commission as general in the army and received a salary from the federal treasury. In response, Lafragua frankly admitted that any intervention on the part of President Lerdo would be viewed unfavorably in Mexico as the government taking sides in the internal affairs of Tamaulipas, specifically in regard to the "personal trouble" Cortina was having with Gov. Servando Canales.[141]

Finally on 1 May 1875, American diplomatic pressure bore fruit. The Mexico City press announced that Cortina had been ordered by telegram to the capital to "give a report on certain affairs on the northern frontier."[142] Realizing what was at stake, Cortina played for time, and when he failed to respond, a second message was sent ordering him to Mexico City. Cortina countered by submitting his resignation from the army, thus removing himself from the authority of the central government. In a game of cat and mouse, President Lerdo refused the resignation and repeated the original order. When Cortina again failed to reply, President Lerdo ordered his arrest.

At La Unión Ranch, three miles above Matamoros, Cortina was apprehended by a Lieutenant Colonel Parrat, acting under orders of Col. José Leonides Cristo of the Mexican military, and was taken to Matamoros where he was held under heavy guard. Because of Cortina's popularity, authorities on both sides of the river were fearful of serious disturbances. Gen. William Tecumseh Sherman, commanding general of the army, reported that stores and residences in Matamoros were closed and that "panic reigns."[143] But although Colonel Cristo was determined to "hold Cortina at all hazards," many residents thought his rescue was only a matter of time.[144] Finally, on the evening of 6 July 1875, Cortina was taken to the mouth of the river at Bagdad and put on the gunboat *Juárez*. He was taken down the coast to tropical Vera Cruz where he was placed on the recently completed Ferrocarril Mexicano and escorted across the Tierra Caliente to Orizaba, then through the Sierra Madre to Puebla and on to Mexico City where he arrived on 24 July 1875.[145]

Hearing that Cortina had been arrested, John Foster rushed to the foreign office to assure Lafragua that the "removal of Cortina would have a great influence in diminishing our troubles."[146] Furthermore, "I expressed to him my

gratification at the arrest of Cortina, and stated that I had no doubt of its benefi-
cial influence, especially if his removal was to be permanent," Foster told
Secretary of State Hamilton Fish.[147] In Texas, Governor Coke was euphoric. Ord,
too, was pleased, content that "some other noted scoundrels" had been taken
also, but fearful also that Cortina would somehow return to the border.[148]

The proclamation that follows was first published in the Mexico City *Monitor
Republicano*, the English-language *Two Eagles*, and finally by the Matamoros
Eco de Ambas Fronteras, a newspaper owned by P. Ramírez and edited by Gil
Vázquez and considered to be Cortina's organ on the border.[149] The lengthy
pronunciamiento was largely a reaction to an article that appeared in the
Mexico City *Sufragio* that praised one of Cortina's political rivals in Tamaulipas,
Andrés Treviño.[150] Initially, Cortina was unaware of the full extent of American
diplomatic pressure on the Lerdo government.

On the border, the *Eco* challenged Cortina's enemies, and pointed out that the
only accusations against Cortina were that he had disobeyed orders. Certain
that he had been "sufficiently punished" by confinement in the prison of
Santiago Tlatelolco on the northern outskirts of Mexico City, the *Eco* was opti-
mistic that Cortina would be "cleared of all charges" and "come once more to
live on this frontier."[151]

When General Ord first received a copy of the proclamation in San Antonio,
he passed it on to Lt. Alfred Maurice Raphall of the 11th Infantry for transla-
tion.[152] Forwarding the pronunciamiento to the army headquarters in Chicago,
Ord saw little more in the document than a "large amount of abuse, recrimina-
tion, and egotism."[153] Nevertheless, Ord was sure that it would appeal to
Cortina's "ignorant and unscrupulous adherents," and he continued to warn
that Cortina was a "bad and dangerous man."[154]

Cortina's pronunciamiento, issued from prison at Santiago Tlatelolco on 20
August 1875, is a desperate cry in the wilderness, a vicious verbal assault on his
political enemies in Matamoros and Tamaulipas. For the historian, the document also contains a biographical sketch of the frontier caudillo that is valuable
in reconstructing large parts of his life.

* * * * * * * * * *

TLATELOLCO PRONUNCIAMIENTO

20 August 1875

EL. C. GRAL. N. CORTINA
AND HIS ACCUSERS BEFORE THE NATION.

"People who live in glass houses should not throw stones."

Averse to taking up public attention with the affairs of my humble person, I have for some time past allowed to pass without notice the attacks of my gratuitous and miserable enemies, because I have always thought that in noticing them I only granted them the attention which is only due to worthy and honorable men; but as in their rancorous attacks they have not confined themselves to drawing down on me the unpopularity and the contempt of the people of Matamoros, (an object which they so much desired,) but have with the tenacity peculiar to the ambitious and perverse deceived the superior government, accumulating against me recriminations emanating from the small and insignificant "Yankeeized ring" residing on the frontier of Tamaulipas, which is, however, very perseveringly hostile to me, and, exaggerating the charges which they present, charged in the nature of diametrically contrary to their true essence, with the definite object of representing me as injurious to that locality, and even the republic, in honor of the truth, and making use of the frank language of the loyal frontier soldier, hard and severe as it may be at the same time on those who have so much malignity, I see myself obliged to answer and wipe away their calumnious imputations.

I am sorry that, in defending myself, it becomes necessary for me to relate facts which I would have left in oblivion if I had not been attacked so rudely by my enemies; but as they, relying on impunity on account of the great distance at which I was from the capital, have endeavored to warp public opinion in a manner unfavorable to me, inventing falsehoods against me, I am going to tear off the mask under which, up to this time, they have concealed themselves, holding up their natural features in this question, which they have raised with a calculated design.

The Treviños and their ring are composed, in great part, of corrupt men, for although among the numbers who compose the Reform or Treviño Club there are honorable exceptions, I repeat, it is mostly composed of servile instruments, who for a handful of lentils sell their conscience and lives, as was seen on the 21st of December 1873, when the directory of the Reform Circle, or Don Andrés Treviño, always ambitious to command, sent to certain disaster the [in]cautious who expected to control by means of pressure the opinions of the population of Matamoros.* But the events that took place then at that time were for Don Andrés and his partisans the hardest and most cruel destruction of their illusions, by Matamoros reminding them that they will never forget those who, in 1851 and 1861, brought fire, death, and pillage to its firesides, and particularly Andrésito, called since that time, or nicknamed, General Firebrand, because, as secretary or soul of Carbajal, he advised those [who] burn[ed] and damage[d] the heroic city, where, if he did not see the light, it is certain that he owes her all that he is.

Behold the reason why the Messrs. Treviño are abhorred in Matamoros, and of their rancor against me! I am sorry that I cannot by an act of magic or legerdemain change in their favor the feelings of that locality, which is justly indignant against those who at two different times have caused its ruin. For this reason, the series of articles which have appeared in the Republican Monitor had not had, in my opinion, and that of sensible persons acquainted with men and things of the frontier, any other object than to procure, by means of lies and false statements, from the superior government the order for the incarceration I am now suffering, which has been given in consequence of the clamor raised against me by my enemies, who are also those of my country, and more particularly yourself, Don Andrésito, since the year 1851.

---

*Andrés Treviño was governor of Tamaulipas at the time of Cortina's raid on Brownsville in 1859. In 1866 Treviño resented Cortina's appointment as governor. He came to control one of the most important political parties in Matamoros and Tamaulipas.

To those like me who know your Machiave[l]lianism and want
of nerve (although a general) to encounter face to face those you
call your enemies, there is nothing surprising to see in the frontier
correspondence published by the Monitor the most terrible
charges against me. The Treviños and some of their adepts, in
accord with their directory residing in this capital, forge their
falsehoods—for what has appeared in the press of this city,
written from here and sent from Matamoros, are nothing else
than falsehoods-with the precise object of exciting against me the
general odium. (In the correspondence in which I am called
without further compliments, a bandit, a robber, an assassin, and
ambitious,) I have never wished to degrade myself by assuming
the role of an accuser. As a public man I have combated my political enemies on legal grounds. To my personal enemies, when I
have not despised them as wretches, I have given the satisfaction
required by decency—to meet charge with charge. I regret very
much to be your enemy, Don Andrésito, but, as I have already
said, it is more important for the public good than for my own
defense that you should be shown up as you are and not with
gilded disguise of wisdom, integrity, and puritanic austerity
which, with as much cynicism as audacity, you wish to put on.

I now proceed to reply to the charges of being a bandit, robber,
assassin, and ambitious man, as they are pleased to style me in
their correspondence. Bandit, because with arms in hand I have
always defended my country in the field of honor, where, be it
said in passing, I have never seen General Andrésito, nor any of
his brothers, certainly because there the precious person of the
first would have been imperiled, which is so much needed in
order that as the most loving son of Mexico, through hatred of the
man that despises him, he should be always seeking the means to
hunt me, alleging falsehoods which may sooner or later, by the
way in which they are presented, cause the evils of which as infa-
mously as gratuitously he pretends to make me the author.

On the northern frontier it is well known while the Americans
of the South, or they that were Confederates, hate me, the origin
of his hatred is a secret from nobody, and particularly for the
Messrs. Treviño, a hatred in which I glory, because I think any
one that is born a Mexican should be proud to contribute or to
have contributed to cause the rights of his fellow-countrymen to

be represented, which have been so often trodden under foot by those who only oppose brute force to justice and reason.

The events of 1859 speak aloud of themselves, and they place me before me of honor, lovers of their country, and of the self-government of peoples, and beyond the reach of your slander and hatred, Messrs. Treviño.

Differing in opinion always respecting the interests of the frontier, and in so marked a manner since I saw myself compelled in Texas to defend the Mexican name, you through a contrary feeling, have been and are constantly on the side of those that ridicule and despise us, for they omit no means, no matter how repugnant, to hold up to the nation as authors of the robberies on both sides of the Rio Grande, Mexicans, of whom I am said to be an accomplice. With respect to this, I will say that it is not so, and that if in Texas robberies of cattle are committed, it is by Americans of Mexican origin, who are tired of suffering vexations and plunderings, of which they have been and are the victims, seeking in this shameful traffic a compensation for their sufferings.

They call me robber, and they do not specify the facts that prove my guilt; for the most that they do it to accuse me of being, at last dates, on the banks of the Río Bravo delivering stock of various brands. It is true that days before my arrest I was in Bagdad, at the mouth of the river of the heroic Matamoros, delivering a herd of 429 cattle of different brands to be taken to Havana. I should not take up my time by answering these secret scandals, but as you, Don Andrésito, endeavor from them to get data to injure me with safety, from the prison in which I now am, I raise my voice that all honorable and impartial men may inform themselves from the citizens Luis Guerra, (the uncle of a certain Don Protasio Guerra, who has declared himself my enemy,) Remigio Chapa, Juan Longoría, and Juan Ayala, as to whose property were the cattle in one of the accusations which the venal press of Matamoros has made against me a few days ago.

But if they do not specify or give any proof of my guilt, I, Don Andrésito, hold you up as the most dexterous sharper in the country and the most able speculator on the national treasury. I will relate the facts in consequence of the filibustering invasion of 1851, in which you and yours were involved. General Avalos ordered that the little property you had should be seized, consisting of a one-story house—which has grown to be a palace by comparison with what it was—a printing-press with old type, and some other trifles, which you, honorable sir, after having received them, caused to be paid you the contemptible sum of $30,000, while they were not worth $500.

In 1853, during the time of the command of General [Adrian] Woll, you obtained, Señor Don Andrés, the order that your property should be returned to you, which was done; and notwithstanding, not to swindle the nation, but as an honorable act and as a signal and patriotic service, you recovered, for your benefit this handsome trifle or drop of water, for which you have been, and very properly, nicknamed El Arrangoiz Fronterizo.* This statement being made, and being proved, as it is, because in this capital are now the persons who took part in the restitution of your property, what must we call a man who claims and receives pay for that which he has not lost? Will you have the goodness to answer this, Señor Treviño; will you do it? I believe it difficult, not to say impossible. I say impossible, because in Tamaulipas when speaking of your memorable administration of two months, it is called the administration of the $40,000, alluding, no doubt, to the celebrated indemnity which forms the greater portion of that sum, unless it be some other $40,000.

Another charge against me is that of assassin, because in the jurisdiction of Reynosa occurred the death of Don Manuel Treviño, originating, according to judicial proof, in his having taken up arms against the officers of justice who were going to arrest him for having committed a violation of the common law.

---

*A French soldier of fortune, Woll had served as a quartermaster under Gen. Santa Anna in 1836 and led the Mexican army that occupied San Antonio in 1842. Serving as governor of Tamaulipas in 1855, he returned to France following the fall of Santa Anna, but later assisted the French in an unsuccessful plot to seize Matamoros. Francisco de Paula Arrangoiz y Berzábal, a leading Santanista and minister of foreign affairs, was blamed for personally profiting from the Treaty of Mesilla (Gadsden Purchase) in 1853. Author of *Méjico desde 1808 hasta 1867*, he was one of the first to suggest to Maximilian that he accept the Mexican throne. Arrangoiz y Berzábal later served the empire as ambassador to Great Britain, Belgium, and the Netherlands, but resigned when he came to realize the extent of church influence on the emperor. He died in Madrid in 1889.

The testimony, in which are some declarations made by relatives of the deceased, which are on file in the papers of the case, gives the lie in the most solemn and positive manner to those who write falsehoods and calumnies in order that men like you, Andrésito, as their organs, may publish them for the patriotic purpose of saving society menaced by me in that count[r]y.

An enlightened statesman like yourself should know that he is the assassin and cruel man who, to show a ridiculous power of authority, gluts his rage on unfortunate men, who led astray and conducted by intriguers into political troubles which we have experienced, shed their blood without any other aspiration or future than being always the victims of ambitious men, and the wall behind which, with more infamy than valor, the wretches, thirsting for gold and power, seek shelter. The pronunciamiento of 1859 in Tampico afforded you, Señor Andrés, an opportunity to show the noble and magnanimous sentiments of your heart. Recollect that at the time unfortunately you were governor you caused to be shot obscure men of the people who, led astray under command of one Mr. Cowley, received a hard lesson in Casa-Mata, all those who were not killed being wounded. For this reason they were taken to the military hospital, from which, after they recovered, by a marked trait of your magnanimous character and philanthropy, they were taken out and executed as they were! And doubtless because in your opinion it was necessary to stain the holy cause of liberty with the blood of unknown men, as were those unfortunates, and above all because it was necessary to make a display of terror, first by disdaining the appeal of the humane citizens of Tampico, who in vain implored mercy for those victims and then ordering officially that all the employees of the custom-house and the State should march in a body to be present at this barbarous act, which at that time justly procured for its author the epithet of "the little Nero of Tamaulipas," which was repeated in chorus by the employees, who openly refused to obey an order so senseless and despotic.

This manner of acting of yours, Señor Don Andrés, being made public, who is it that deserves most justly the pompous title of assassin, which you and yours have so generously bestowed upon me? It is true I have ordered the executions of chiefs who have caused the troops to rebel that were under my command,

and when I ordered such executions I obeyed the articles of war applicable to representative men, and not to the simple men of the people. And now lay your hand on your heart, and in all sincerity, if your soul is still susceptible of it, answer me who is the assassin.

It remains now for me to answer the last charge made against me, of being ambitious—doubtless on account of my position of general in the army. But if I wear the sash of a brigadier, I did not obtain it by palace intrigues, but for the following services, that I will lightly sketch. Although absolutely ignorant of military service, nevertheless, from my early youth, I bore arms in the difficult and dangerous struggle against Indians, defending my rancho and the interests of my family. Judging me to be experienced in this sort of warfare, the frontiersmen of the north, in 1859, confided to me their great cause in critical times, as I will show. After the war with the United States and the conclusion of the treaties of Guadalupe Hidalgo and of the Mesilla, by which was sold to the nation two-thirds of the national territory for a mess of pottage, the execution of Article 11 of said treaty of Guadalupe stipulated in favor of the frontier having been remitted to the American Government, the subornation of the frontier States having been squandered, and a yoke of iron imposed on them by the Yankee police by said treaties, those unfortunate inhabitants saw themselves abandoned by their own government, tyrannized over, despoiled of everything, and destined by their new conqueror to be the helots of America, or the slaves of their slaves. So it is, seeing themselves outlawed, and becoming desperate, they saw no other future than that of the damned of Dante, written on the gates of his empire, "Abandon all Hope!" But at supreme moments the saying of O'Connell is verified, "Peoples, like men, situated in extreme cases, profit by the opportunities offered by God."*

This is what happened to these unfortunates, who in those solemn moments believed me to be the instrument destined by Providence to save them.

---

*Probably a quote by Daniel O'Connell (1775-1847), a Catholic Irish statesman who is considered to have been the single greatest influence on the emergence of Irish political nationalism in the nineteenth century.

In effect, in about the middle of 1859, I went to Brownsville, and being at a cafe, I saw that an American sheriff was dragging off a poor Mexican by the collar. Indignantly I asked him, "Why do you ill-treat this man?" He answered me insolently, and then I punished his insolence and avenged my countrymen by shooting him with a pistol and stretching him at my feet. Immediately I mounted my horse, with my protege behind me, and withdrew amidst the stupor of the Yankees and the enthusiastic hurrahs of the Mexicans. From that moment the Texas Mexicans proclaimed and recognized me as the chief, and with those valiant patriots, after having twice defeated considerable Yankee parties sent to arrest me, I took Brownsville, proclaiming victoriously the Mexican Republic, and chastising its enemies.

Being attached afterward by superior forces, I was obliged to cross to the Mexican side of the Bravo, where I owed my safety to the asylum given me in the Sierrita by my relative, General D. José María J. Carvajal, commanding general at that time of the Rojo army in Tamaulipas. You, Don Andrés, being governor of that State, gave repeated orders that the forces of Matamoros crossing the line should join the American forces to follow me up to extermination, as a bandit and filibuster, an order in which you have gloried always as a trait of your high policy, which to this day is followed up against me with the vindictive ardor of that time.

Being in condition and re-enforced in Tamaulipas, I joined General Comonfort in his passage through this State toward the interior, and I accompanied him with my force, where his division received orders to operate in conjunction with the general-in-chief of the army of the east in the neighborhood of Pueblo, when in May, 1863, we defeated the French at San Lorenzo and other points, until we retired after the disastrous surrender of that place.* Returning to Tamaulipas at the end of 1863 and the beginning of 1864, I succeeded in terminating the civil war in the State between Rojos and Crinolinos in favor of the superior government.

By this service, a commission as governor of Tamaulipas made out in your favor remained without effect, and, in spite of all you could do, could not be enforced in Matamoros, I being appointed

*See note on page 53.

general governor and commanding-general of said State, and
presented by the city of Matamoros, through its illustrious
common council, with a sword of honor. When Vidaurri, in
concert with other generals, abandoned the government of the
citizen President Juárez, I was his principal support, without
which his ruin was inevitable, accompanied by grave, if not
irreparable, prejudice to the national cause. When the general
government retired as far as Paso del Norte, I found myself
compelled to serve the empire for a time, to save some forces and
to preserve for the republic the troops of our command, which I
succeeded in doing, for shortly after, with that force, I combated
the empire in the center of Tamaulipas, and at the siege and
taking of Matamoros, of Mexico, and Querétaro, when was
consolidated the independence of Mexico by the taking and
shooting of Maximilian, who I and General [Ramón] Corona
captured on the 15th of May, 1867. In 1871, I contributed to save
the general government at Lo de Obejo, Tetela del Oro, and other
points.* Latterly, my presence on the frontier has maintained
peace with the United States and the autonomy of Tamaulipas,
for which the people of Matamoros have honored me by electing
me for the past and present year as mayor.

Can you, Don Andrés, present better or even equal services to
justify your grade of general? You are neither a practical nor a
scientific general, and, rack your brain as you will, your list of
services, none but the following campaigns are found: In
September, 1851, your pronunciamiento de la loba, bringing with
you Yankees and foreigners to oppress and lay waste our
country.** At the same date your attack of Matamoros, where
were burned and sacked more than two hundred houses, from
which sacking (according to public voice and report) you
adjudged to yourself and family upward of $200,000, the origin of
your fortune, which your brother Don Manuel has employed in

---

*Corona had been minister of war in 1859 and was second in command to General Escobedo at
the siege of Querétaro in 1867.

**At La Loba near Guerrero, upriver from Camargo, on 3 September 1851, José María Canales,
son of Antonio Canales and brother of Servando Canales, wrote up a revolutionary plan in an
attempt to force a free trade zone along the Rio Grande. The plan's principal instigator, José
María Carvajal, had strong ties and financial backing from several Anglo-Texans, especially the
Brownsville business establishment. Leading an army against Matamoros, Carvajal failed in
what has been called the Merchants War.

commerce. In 1859 your famous order that the troops at the Bravo united with the Americans to pursue me to extermination as a bandit and filibuster for having defended the cause of Mexico. The drop of water, the $30,000. The execution of the unfortunates at Casa Mata, in Tampico, after taking them from the military hospital on their recovery. In 1861, the new attack on Matamoros, equal to that of 1851. The continued recommendations to your brother, the Mexican consul, that he should announce the depredations of Mexicans on points in Texas, (attributing them to my employees,) while he scarcely ever notifies the government of the marauding, smuggling, and cattle-stealing of Americans on Mexican territory. The constant claiming of credits against the treasury, (some, and important ones, already paid,) perhaps without the legal voucher from the custom-house, like the $30,000 already mentioned. Your monomania to be governor of Tamaulipas, supported by your club correspondence in newspapers; and now your accusation against me as being an instrument of Yankee policy! *"Sic itur ad astra!"* [This is the way to the stars!]

In the presence of these services, tendered, respectively, by each of us, I believe, if you still dare to call me ambitious, your own conscience, as well as the nation, would answer, saying, if Cortina has ambition, it is legitimate, as being inspired by the love of glory, and based on positive services rendered to his country and humanity, which is the ambition of great men. But that of Señor Treviño is spurious, being inspired by the morbid desire to cut a figure, and based on court intrigues, when not on reprehensive actions, which is that of the worshipers of the golden calf and of mammon, who sacrifice their country and humanity for their private interests. Such is the judgment, without appeal, which contemporaneous history pronounces on my service and yours, Andrésito! and his judgment is confirmed by Tamaulipas in respect to you, by calling you *"El hijo de la loba!"* (the son of the wolf). This nickname shows their appreciation of all your ambition. In one particular you were born into the political world from the plan *"de la loba,"* according to which its author, to satisfy ambition, did not hesitate to profane the sacred soil of their country with the foul foot of the Yankee and the foreigner, who would lacerate her breast. In the second place, they find an analogy between you and the son of another she-wolf in Rome, the celebrated Romulus, a monster of ambition, since it makes him kill his brother Remus, the Roman people, and forge chains to fetter the universe, until the very senate see themselves obliged, in an ovación, to kill and quarter him secretly, each senator carrying off under his cloak a piece of his palpitating members, to do away with this plague of humanity, telling the people, "After that his father, the god Mars, satisfied with the glory of his son, had raised him to Olympus, placing him along the immortals." Who, then, is now the ambitious man?

By what I have shown, it is evident that Yankee influence, if not the Government of the United States, wishes, at any cost, to make its expiatory victim of the man who in September, 1859, solemnly proclaimed in Brownsville the sacred cause of Mexico, giving effect to the energetic protest of the States of Tamaulipas and Coahuila against the treaty of Guadalupe Hidalgo, being since that time the most constant defender of that cause on the frontier, and not having being seen that time the most constant defender of that wish from the strong government of Benito Juárez, who successfully struggled against three great powers, now endeavor to obtain from the present cabinet, through an accuser and its old ally, the son of the plan "De la Loba," Don Andrés Treviño. That this general believing himself, no doubt, the bravest of the brave, on account of his exploits at Matamoros, has not calculated sufficiently the effect of his injurious accusations, since it is at least prudent for those that live in glass houses not to throw stones; that, believing himself the invulnerable Achilles of Tamaulipas, he has left uncovered the heel where he could be wounded, and believing himself to be the Bayard of the frontier, or the knight without fear and without reproach, has declared with a blanched face before the nation, that he will never cover himself under the veil of the anonymous (as in his correspondence from Matamoros), but that henceforth all his articles against me will appear signed with his name, indicating in this way clearly that he will continue, as he has done heretofore, his favorite system of calling calumnies facts, positive, incontrovertible, and held for certain by public opinion, when they are against him, and on the contrary facts proven, authentic, and even evangelical, the low calumnies invented by him and his partner in this capital, and published by his official or venal press of Matamoros, against my reputation and good name.

But I trust that the people of the Mexican Republic, the government of the State of Tamaulipas, and the illustrious common council of the loyal and heroic Matamoros, seeing themselves attacked in my person, will take up my accusation against this Faust of Matamoros, seduced by the Mephistopheles of the United States.* But as far as Señor Treviño is concerned, without fearing his celebrity, without his chivalrous protection, and without losing sight of his vulnerable parts, I will only imitate him by subscribing my vindicatory articles with my own name, since, being brought into a close field in which the jewel is worn unto death, I promise that I will only combat in this barrier in a fair fight—that is to say, with the arms of the law, on the ground of reason, under the banner of patriotism, with the consciousness of justice and with faith in my good cause. Such has been my course in relating undoubted facts in this article, and such it will be in exposing other facts, which doubtless I will still have to related in succeeding articles of this controversy, facts for which doubtless, Don Andrésito will not give me a vote of thanks, but the word is already pronounced, and no human power is able to oppose successfully its irresistible truth, without changing the essence of things, which by its nature is immutable. It is now, then, for the high, righteous, and irreversible judgment of the nation to decide between the humble prisoner of Santiago and his powerful adversary of the court.

Santiago, Tlatelolco, August 20, 1875.

JUAN N. CORTINA

---

*According to legend, Dr. Johann Faustus, a learned sixteenth century fortune-teller and magician, sold his soul to the devil (Mephistopheles) in exchange for youth, knowledge, and magical powers. This story inspired Johann Wolfgang von Goethe's masterpiece *Faust*.

9

Cortina's pronunciamiento of 18 May 1876 follows his imprisonment in Mexico City by Pres. Sebastián Lerdo de Tejada eleven months earlier. From the village of Azcapotzalco, fewer than four miles northwest of Mexico City, where Cortina was under house arrest, he defiantly announced his support of Gen. Porfirio Díaz and the Plan de Tuxtepec.

In March 1876, five years after his unsuccessful attempt to overthrow Benito Juárez under the Plan de la Noria, Díaz had issued his Plan de Tuxtepec, accusing Lerdo of violating the sovereignty of the states and municipalities and squandering government money. More importantly, the plan called for a law that would prevent the reelection of the president and governors.[155] Whether Cortina was ideologically attracted to the Plan de Tuxtepec or simply saw it as an opportunity to escape from Mexico City is uncertain.

In any event, shortly after leaving Mexico City, Cortina joined a force of Porfiristas but was turned back at Ajuchitlan in the state of Hidalgo by a much larger Lerdista army.[156] Defeated again in San Luis Potosí two weeks later, he struck out for the border, there to recruit men under the banner of General Díaz.[157]

A copy of Cortina's pronunciamiento survived when John W. Foster, minister to Mexico, clipped a copy from the Mexico City *Two Eagles* and sent it to the United States secretary of state, Hamilton Fish, in Washington, D.C.[158] The proclamation was probably translated at the office of the *Two Eagles* by either George W. Clarke, the editor, or J. Mastella Clarke, assistant editor.

* * * * * * * * * *

PRONUNCIAMIENTO

AZCAPOTZALCO

18 May 1876

GEN. JUAN N. CORTINA TO THE NATION

FELLOW-CITIZENS: Ten months ago the despotic government of D. Sebastián Lerdo de Tejada tore me from my home, where I lived quietly at the side of my family, availing itself, for this purpose, of mean and miserable calumnies, which, desiring to give a varnish of legality to an act really unauthorized by law, the government itself put in circulation. Six months I was in prison in the capital of the republic, pending the investigations which were being instituted, and from which the government could not do less than desist, convinced of the fruitless result of its perverse machinations.

The trial being abandoned, I was taken out of prison, the minister of war ordering me to remain in the capital, where I spent three months more, subject to an excessive surveillance from the police, and with the restriction that I should not go even a league from the city.

This unjustifiable excess of arbitrary acts exercised against me had no other origin than the caprice of the government, which, knowing my integrity, understood that it could at no time rely upon me to make me its accomplice in the efforts for the re-election to which it aspires with entire disregard of the unanimous will of the people, who reject it.

Now that I have succeeded in freeing myself from the clutches of the tyrant and in regaining my liberty, I earnestly protest before the nation against the outrages committed upon my person by the arbitrary government of Sebastián Lerdo de Tejada, and I assure you also that I will be, as ever, the defender of the guarantees which the constitution of '57 concedes to the people, and which the Plan of Tuxtepec, proclaimed by the well-merited citizen, Gen. Porfirio Díaz, seeks to make effective, which plan I accept and second in all its parts, and will defend at all cost.

I invite, in the name of the public liberties, all Mexicans who love their institutions, and who in other times fought with me in defense of liberty, to rally around the flag which is unfurled by the well-merited General Porfirio Díaz, because it is the symbol of the constitution of '57, under whose shade alone can be given to the people of Mexico a truly republican government.

Viva la constitución de '57! Viva el Ciudadano General Porfirio Díaz, su defensor! Free suffrage and the constitution!

JUAN N. CORTINA

This photograph of Cortina with his third wife, María de Jesús López, was prob-
ably taken in Mexico City a few years before his death. Cortina had married a first
cousin, María Dolores Tijerina, in Matamoros in July of 1846, and in January of
1850, after the death of his first wife, wed Rafaela Cortez in Brownsville's
Immaculate Conception Church. (University of Texas, Latin American Collection)

10

Following his Azcapotzalco pronunciamiento on 18 May 1876, Cortina spent only a short time with the Porfiristas in Central Mexico. By early May 1876, he had arrived at his Rancho del Canelo some sixty miles from Matamoros, where he began to recruit men for an attack on the federal forces in Matamoros. By 6 July, Thomas F. Wilson, the American consul in Matamoros, was reporting that Cortina, with seven hundred men, had advanced to within fifteen miles of the town.[159] Fearful of Cortina's return to the border, American authorities contemplated intervening to stop him. The commander of the gunboat *Río Bravo*, along with the Texas Rangers, went as far as to conspire to start a war on the river.[160]

By December, Cortina had driven the federal forces from Reynosa, Camargo, and Mier, but Matamoros held out. Although he was determined to take the town, it was another Díaz general, Miguel Blanco, who entered Matamoros first. By marching directly from Mexico City, Blanco reached the border on 14 February 1877 and assumed command of all Díaz forces on the Rio Grande frontier. Two days later, Cortina arrived with one thousand men "amid the ringing of the church bells and other demonstrations of general rejoicing."[161] Consul Wilson recorded that Cortina was received on the main plaza "with all the military honors becoming the occasion."[162] General Blanco was there to read a proclamation congratulating Cortina and his men for their "heroic conduct." Consul Wilson, always with a keen eye on Cortina, wrote Washington: "The partisans of Cortina again occupy all the civil and many of the military offices on the frontier of the lower Rio Grande and Cortina himself is possessed of as much influence and authority as at any time within the past ten years."[163]

Cortina died of pneumonia in the village of Azcapotzalco near Mexico City on 30 October 1894 and was buried in the Panteón de Dolores. (Editor's photo)

Little did Cortina know that his return to the border was to be brief. With his bitter rival, Servando Canales, as governor of Tamaulipas, Díaz realized that two caudillos fighting a bloody war for power on the Rio Grande could only weaken his government. Furthermore, the United States continued to withhold diplomatic recognition of the Díaz regime until Díaz could put an end to the cattle raids on the border.

Shortly after Cortina rode victoriously into Matamoros, a telegram arrived ordering him to Mexico City. Then, as he had attempted to do with President Lerdo two years earlier, he stalled for time. But on 24 February 1877, Governor Canales ordered General Blanco to arrest and imprison him.[164] The following day Governor Canales entered Matamoros at the head of a large army and assumed command of the frontier while Blanco "hastily left" and "took refuge in Brownsville."[165]

Within days Canales had assembled a general military court to try Cortina; with Canales possessing a long and bitter hatred of Cortina, the verdict was a foregone conclusion. On 28 February 1877, Consul Wilson informed Washington that it was "presumed that Cortina's trial will result in his being shot and his large estates confiscated."[166] Indeed, on 10 April, the court found Cortina guilty and sentenced him to death.[167]

John S. Ford would later take credit for saving Cortina's life. Ford crossed the river to meet personally with Canales and tell the governor that if Cortina were executed, history would record "that personal ill feeling actuated your approval."[168] Canales evidently agreed and decided to send Cortina to Mexico City where Díaz could decide his fate. On 9 April, with his army now disbanded, Cortina was taken under a heavy guard to the mouth of the river where Díaz had sent the steamer *Independencia* to carry him to Vera Cruz.[169]

Arriving in Mexico City, Cortina was again placed in the prison of Santiago Tlatelolco.[170] He would remain in prison, often in bad health, or under house arrest at the village of Azcapotzalco, for the next sixteen years until his death on 30 October 1894. The pronunciamiento that follows, issued by Cortina upon his entry into Matamoros on 16 February 1877, was sent by Thomas Wilson to Washington and today is in the National Archives.

* * * * * * * * * *

PRONUNCIAMIENTO
H. Matamoros
16 February 1877

Gen. Juan N. Cortina to Brigade
of National Guard under his command

Comrades in Arms:

The reason that obliged you to raise arms against a tyrannical
and corrupt government exists no more.

The cause which you supported with constance and valor has
been crowned with a most complete triumph, and consequently,
public freedom has been salvaged. The country should no longer,
and could no longer maintain an overgrown army; as much, the
Supreme government of the Republic allows you to go to the
bosom of your domestic household to rest from the fatigues of
war and to amend by hard work those prejudices suffered for our
interests.

I am departing to take care of business of public interest with
the National Government. During my stay in the capital, I will
acknowledge your services and abnegation before the Supreme
Magistrate of the Republic, for which you will be rewarded with
worthy recognition.

In bidding farewell, I thank you for the perseverance with
which you accompanied me during such honorable as well as
lengthy campaign, and urge you to remain close to the authorities in support of the strife to ensure order and public tranquility
and to continue being good sons of a frontier, those who are
always willing to sacrifice themselves for their country's liberty
and institutions.

Juan N. Cortina

ENDNOTES

INTRODUCTION

1 Stephen B. Oates, ed., John Salmon Ford, *Rip Ford's Texas* (Austin: University of Texas Press, 1963), 261-62.

2 Ibid.

3 Ibid.

4 Ibid., 281-82n, 351.

5 Ibid., 412.

6 Ibid., 413-14.

7 Ibid., 285-86.

8 J. Frank Dobie, *A Vaquero of the Brush Country* (Austin: University of Texas Press, 1985).

9 Ibid., xii, 50.

10 Walter Prescott Webb, *The Texas Rangers: A Century of Frontier Defense* (Austin: University of Texas Press, 1965), 176.

11 Ibid., 176-77.

12 Lyman L. Woodman, *Cortina, The Rogue of the Rio Grande* (San Antonio: Naylor Co., 1950), 2,8.

13 Ibid., 8.

14 Ibid., 9.

15 Charles W. Goldfinch, *Juan N. Cortina, 1824-1892: A Re-Appraisal* (Chicago, 1947), 10-11, 15.

16 Ibid., 44.

17 J. Fred Rippy, "Border Troubles Along the Rio Grande, 1848-1860," *Southwestern Historical Quarterly,* 23 (October 1919): 93.

18 Goldfinch, *Cortina: A Re-Appraisal,* 59.

19 Ibid., 67. Also, Carey McWilliams, *North From Mexico, The Spanish Speaking People of the United States* (New York: Greenwood Press, 1968), 106-8, 126.

20 Ibid.

21 Pedro Castillo and Alberto Camarillo, *Furia y Muerte: Los Bandidos Chicanos* (Los Angeles: Aztlán Publications, 1973), 85-112.

22 Eric J. Hobsbaum, *Primitive Rebels: Studies in Archaic Forms of Social Movements in the 19th and 20th Centuries* (New York: Fredrick A. Praeger, 1959).

23 Arnoldo De León, *They Called Them Greasers: Anglo Attitudes Towards Mexicans in 19th Century Texas* (Austin: University of Texas Press, 1983), 53-55, 83-85.

24 Robert J. Rosenbaum, *Mexicano Resistance in the Southwest, "The Sacred Right of Self-Preservation"* (Austin: University of Texas Press, 1981), 42.

25 Carlos Larralde, "Beyond Banditry: The Cortinista Movement of 1848-1876," 4, 11. Unpublished article courtesy of the author. See also: Carlos Larralde, *Mexican American Movements and Leaders* (Los Alamitos, Calif.: Hwong Publishing Co., 1976).

26 Michael G. Webster, "Texas Manifest Destiny and the Mexican Border Conflict, 1865-1880." Ph.D. diss., Indiana University, 1972.

27 James Ridley Douglas, "Juan Cortina: El Caudillo de la Frontera." M.A. thesis, University of Texas, 1987.

28 Ibid., 130.

29 Ibid., 131.

30 Ibid., 132.

31 Ibid., 94.

32 Mirabel Miro Flaquer, ed., *Catálogo de Documentos—Carta de la Collección Porfirio Díaz, Tamaulipas, Marzo 1876-Noviembre 1885* (Ciudad Victoria: Universidad Autónoma de Tamaulipas, 1985), vols. 1 and 2.

33   Larry McMurtry, *Lonesome Dove* (New York: Simon & Schuster, 1985), 111. Also, Larry McMurtry to Mr. Freling, 15 April 1989, in "Archie P. McDonald: Personal Reflections," Re. Arts & Letters 17 (Spring 1991): 41-46.

34   McMurtry, *Lonesome Dove*, 118.

35   James A. Michener, *Texas* (Random House: New York, 1985), 561-62.

36   Mexico City *La Patria*, 1 November 1894; *San Antonio Daily Express*, 2, 3 November 1894; *Brownsville Daily Herald*, 5 November 1894.

PRONUNCIAMIENTOS

1: PRONUNCIAMIENTO, RANCHO DEL CARMEN, 30 SEPTEMBER 1859

37   List of Candidates Qualifying, 14 September 1854, Cameron County, Record Group 307, Texas State Archives (TSA), Austin; Commissioner's Court Minutes (1848-1862), Cameron County, County Clerk's Office, Brownsville, 15; Minutebook 1 (1850-1859), City Secretary's Office, Brownsville, 123, 346-47. Sometime after the Civil War, the family began using Glavecke instead of Glaevecke.

38   7th Census (1850), Cameron County, NA.

39   *Antonio Tijerina vs. Adolphus Glaevecke*, Cause no. 549, Minutebook B, District Clerk's Office, Brownsville, 577-79.

40   Adolphus Glarvke *(sic)* Affidavit, 16 January 1860, *Difficulties on the Southwestern Frontier*, 36th Cong., 1st sess., no. 52, 65. This set of records will hereafter be referred to as DSF. Also, W. W. Nelson, Indictments by the Spring 1859 District Court of the 12th Judicial District, Sam Houston Papers, TSA; Ford, *Rip Ford's Texas*, 262-63.

41   Juan N. Cortina to the Public, 8 September 1875, *Texas Frontier Troubles*, 44th Cong., 1st sess., no. 343, 117-18. This set of records will hereafter be referred to as TFT.

42   Robert Shears Affidavit, 14 January 1860, *Hostilities on the Rio Grande*, 36th Cong., 1st sess., no. 21, 17. This set of records will hereafter be referred to as HRG.

43   W. P. Reyburn to F. A. Hatch, 21 November 1859, *DSF*, 65.

44   S. P. Heintzelman to Robert E. Lee, 1 March 1860, *TTF*, 3-4; *State of Texas vs. Juan Nepomuceno Cortina, et al.*, November 1859, Washington Daniel Miller Papers, TSA.

45   A. Werbeskie Affidavit, 10 January 1860, *HRG*, 12.

46   Charles W. Goldfinch and José T. Canales, *Juan N. Cortina: Two Interpretations* (New York: Arno Press, 1974), 39. The idea that José María "was responsible for the wording of Cortina's first proclamation" was that of Herbert Davenport, Goldfinch reported.

47   W. P. Reyburn to F. A. Hatch, 21 November 1859, *DSF*, 65; List of Candidates Qualifying, 4 August 1856, Cameron County, RG 307, TSA; Commissioner's Court Minutes (1848-1862), County Clerk's Office, 290.

48   [Richard] Fitzpatrick to Lewis Cass, 4 January 1860, Matamoros Despatches, RG 59, National Archives (NA).

49   Matamoros *El Jayne*, 12 October 1859, quoted in *Reports of the Committee of Investigations Sent in 1873 by the Mexican Government to the Frontier of Texas* (New York: Baker & Godwin, 1875), 136.

2: PRONUNCIAMIENTO, RANCHO DEL CARMEN, 23 NOVEMBER 1859

50   Francis W. Latham to David E. Twiggs, 28 September 1859, *DSF*, 21-22.

51   Henry Webb, et al., to Hardin R. Runnels, 2 October 1859, *DSF*, 21.

52   Ibid.

53   Ibid.

54   Stephen Powers to James Buchanan, 18 October 1859, *DSF*, 35.

55   S. P. Heintzelman to Robert E. Lee, 1 March 1860, *TTF*, 3-4.

56   S. P. Heintzelman to John Withers, 1 March 1860, *TTF*, 4. Cabrera was later hanged by the Texas Rangers.

57   W. B. Thompson to Stephen Powers and J. B. Brown[e], 25 October 1859, *DSF*; Brownsville *Fort Brown Flag*, extra, 29 October 1859, in *DSF*, 44-45; Israel B. Bigelow, letter, 1 November 1859, in *Galveston News*, quoted in *DSF*, 48-49; Brownsville *Evening Ranchero*, 5 July 1876, in W. H. Chatfield, *Twin Cities of the Border and the Country of the Lower Rio Grande* (New Orleans: E. P. Brandao, 1893), 13.

58   S. P. Heintzelman to Robert E. Lee, 1 March 1860, *TTF*, 3-4.

59   Rosenbaum, *Mexican Resistance in the Southwest*, 44.

60   Ibid. Rosenbaum draws the same conclusion.

61   Broadside, 26 November 1859, in LR, AGO, RG 94, NA. The pronunciamiento was also published in the Corpus Christi *Ranchero*, 3 December 1859.

62   Ibid.

3: PRONUNCIAMIENTO, MATAMOROS, 8 NOVEMBER 1863

63   Jerry Thompson, *Mexican Texans in the Union Army* (El Paso: Texas Western Press, 1986), 8-12.

64   Juan N. Cortina to John L. Haynes, 12 September 1863, letter in author's collection.

65   N. P. Banks to Charles P. Stone, 2 November 1863, *The War of the Rebellion: A Compilation of the Official Records of the Union and Confederate Armies* (Washington: Government Printing Office, 1889), ser. 1, vol. 26, pt. 1:396. These voluminous records will hereafter be referred to as *O.R.*

66   Ibid., 398.

67   N. P. Banks to H. W. Halleck, 6 November 1863, *O.R.*, 1, 26, 1:399-400.

68   Ibid.

69   Ibid.

70   Ibid.

71   H. P. Bee to Edmund P. Turner, 8 November 1863, *O.R.*, 1. 26, 1:434-35.

72   Richard Taylor to James Duff, 3 November 1863, *O.R.*, 1, 26, 1:434-44.

73   H. P. Bee to Edmund P. Turner, 8 November 1863, *O.R.*, 1, 26, 1:434-35.

74   N. P. Banks to H. W. Halleck, 6 November 1863, *O.R.*, 1, 26, 1:399-400; J. A. Quintero to J. P. Benjamin, 26 November 1863, Pickett Papers, Library of Congress, Washington, D.C. For Cobos as a bandit chief, see: Paul J. Vanderwood, *Disorder and Progress: Bandits, Police and Mexican Development* (Lincoln: University of Nebraska Press, 1981), 3-4.

75   Milo Kearney and Anthony Knopp, *Boom and Bust: The Historical Cycles of Matamoros and Brownsville* (Austin: Eakin Press, 1991), 127-28.

76   José María Cobos to his Companions in Arms, 6 November 1863, *O.R.*, 1, 26, 1:401.

77   N. P. Banks to H. W. Halleck, 6 November 1863, *O.R.*, 1, 16, 1:399-400.

78   Ibid. Also, Nannie M. Tilley, ed., *Federals on the Frontier: The Diary of Benjamin F. McIntyre, 1862-1864* (Austin: University of Texas Press, 1963), 388-89; Santiago Vidaurri to Benito Juárez, 7 November 1863, *Benito Juárez: Documentos, Discursos y Correspondencia* (Mexico City: Secretaria del Patrimonio Nacional, 1964-69), 8:315; James W. Daddysman, *The Matamoros Trade: Confederate Commerce, Diplomacy and Intrigue* (Cranbury, N. J.: University of Delaware Press, 1984), 94-95.

79   N. P. Banks to H. W. Halleck, 6 November 1863, *O.R.*, 1, 16, 1:399-400.

80   Juan Nepomuceno Cortina to the Public, 8 November 1863, enclosed with N. P. Banks to H. W. Halleck, 8 November 1863, *O.R.*, 1, 26, 1:406-7.

4: PRONUNCIAMIENTO, H. MATAMOROS, 14 JANUARY 1864

81   F. J. Herron to Charles P. Stone, 16 January 1864, *O.R.*, 1, 34, 2:92-93.

82   Tilley, *Federals on the Frontier*, 290.

83   N. J. T. Dana to Charles P. Stone, 11 December 1863, *O.R.*, 1, 26, 1:843-44.

84   N. J. T. Dana to Charles P. Stone, 18 December 1863, *O.R.*, 1, 26, 1:864-65.

85   Tilley, *Federals on the Frontier*, 290.

86   F. J. Herron to Charles P. Stone, 16 January 1864, *O.R.*, 1, 34, 2:92. Also, Daddysman, *The*

Matamoros Trade, 96.

87   Tilley, *Federals on the Frontier*, 290.

88   Manuel Ruiz to Benito Juárez, 12 January 1864, *Correspondencia de Juárez*, 8:533-34.

89   Tilley, *Federals on the Frontier*, 290.

90   Ibid. Also, F. J. Herron to Charles P. Stone, 16 January 1864, *O.R.*, 1, 34, 2:92.

91   *Frank Leslie's Illustrated Newspaper*, 20 February 1864; F. J. Herron to Charles P. Stone, 15 January 1864, *O.R.*, 1, 34, 1:84; Houston *Tri-Weekly Telegraph*, 1 February 1864.

92   L. Pierce, Jr., to F. J. Herron, 12 January 1864, *O.R.*, 1, 34, 1:81.

93   Ibid.

94   Ibid.

95   Manuel Ruiz to F. J. Herron, 12 January 1864, *Correspondencia de Juárez*, 8:535. This same letter is in *O.R.*, 1, 34, 1:82.

96   F. J. Herron to Charles P. Stone, 15 January 1864, *O.R.*, 1, 34, 1:82.

97   F. J. Herron to Manuel Ruiz, 12 January 1864, *O.R.*, 1, 34, 1:82-83.

98   H. Bertram to Herron, 12 [13] January 1864, *O.R.*, 1, 34, 1:83.

99   Ibid.

100 Tillie, *Federals on the Frontier*, 292.

101 Ibid.

102 F. J. Herron to Charles P. Stone, 15 January 1864, *O.R.*, 1, 34, 1:84.

103 Manuel Ruiz to Benito Juárez, 14 January 1864, *Correspondencia de Juárez*, 8:536-37.

104 Juan N. Cortina to the Inhabitants of Matamoros, 14 January 1864, *Correspondencia de Juárez*, 8:538-39.

5: PRONUNCIAMIENTO, HEROIC MATAMOROS, 27 FEBRUARY 1864

105 Juan N. Cortina to Santiago Vidaurri, 28 December 1863, Correspondencia de Santiago Vidaurri, Archivo General del Estado de Nuevo León, Monterrey, Mexico.

106 Charles Allen Smart, *Viva Juárez: A Biography* (New York: J. B. Lippincott, 1963), 277; Ralph Roeder, *Juárez and his Mexico* (New York: Viking Press, 1947), 512-13.

107 J. A. Quintero to J. P. Benjamin, 25 January 1864, Pickett Papers; Ronnie Tyler, S*antiago Vidaurri and the Southern Confederacy* (Austin: Texas State Historical Association, 1973), 137.

108 Juan N. Cortina to Benito Juárez, 21 January 1864, *Correspondencia de Juárez*, 8:549.

109 Juan N. Cortina to Benito Juárez, 6 February 1864, *Correspondencia de Juárez*, 8:556-57.

110 Juan N. Cortina to Benito Juárez, 25 February 1864, *Correspondencia de Juárez*, 8:557-58.

111 Smart, Viva Juárez, 303; Tyler, *Santiago Vidaurri and the Southern Confederacy*, 139.

112 Tyler, S*antiago Vidaurri and the Southern Confederacy*, 139. Vidaurri later became minister of finance in Maximilian's Council of State and was captured and shot without trial in Mexico City on 8 July 1867.

113 Ibid.

6: BIOGRAPHY, MEXICO CITY, JULY 1870

114 The biography was published in the 24, 27, 29 September and 1 October 1879 issues in the *Daily Ranchero*.

115 Count Emile de Kératry, *The Rise and Fall of the Emperor Maximilian, A Narrative of the Mexican Empire, 1861-67 from Authentic Documents with the Imperial Correspondence* (London: Sampson Low, Son, and Marston, 1868). For the French edition, see: *L'Empereur Maximilien, son eleva-tion et sa chute* (Paris, 1867). See also, Le Cte. E. De Kératry, *La créance Jecker, les indemnités francaises el les emprunts mexicain*s (Paris, 1868).

116 Brownsville *Daily Ranchero*, 24 September 1870.

117 Kératry, *The Rise and Fall of Maximilian*, 70.

118 Ibid.

119 Brownsville *Daily Ranchero*, 24 September 1870.

120 Ibid.

121 Brownsville *Daily Ranchero,* 24 September 1870.

122 Maltby had started the *Ranchero* in Corpus Christi before the Civil War but had moved the press to Santa Margarita temporarily in January 1864 to avoid the Federal occupation of the Texas coast. Maltby next took the press to Matamoros and after the Civil War moved to Brownsville in December 1865. Shortly thereafter he again resumed publication in Matamoros but by September 1866 the *Ranchero* was back in Brownsville. A. A. Champion and Vivian Kearney, "Papers and Personalities of Frontier Journalism (1830s to 1890s)" in *More Studies in Brownsville History,* ed. Milo Kearney (Brownsville: Pan American University at Brownsville, 1989), 112-61.

7: PRONUNCIAMIENTO, H. MATAMOROS, 19 SEPTEMBER 1870

123 Kearney and Knopp, *Boom and Bust,* 136.

124 Ibid.

125 Ibid.

126 Kératry, *La Contre-Guérilla Francaise Au Mexique,* 191-99.

127 M. Escobedo to the Minister of War and Marine, 16 June 1866; Escobedo to same, 20 June 1866, both in *Conditions of Affairs in Mexico,* 39th Cong., 2d sess., no. 1294, 226-29. Also, Juan Fidel Zorrilla, *Gobernadores, Obispos y Rectores* (Ciudad Victoria: Universidad Autónoma de Tamaulipas, 1979), 22-23.

128 Agreement for the Surrender of Matamoros, ibid., 223.

129 See pronunciamiento no. 5. Also, Matamoros *Eco de Ambas Fronteras,* 8 October 1875, in LR, AGO, 1875, RG 94, NA, published in TFT, 115-19.

130 Mexico City *Two Eagles,* 25 June 1870; Brownsville *Daily Ranchero,* 27 May 1870.

131 Brownsville *Daily Ranchero,* 14 July 1870.

132 Ibid., 22 September 1870.

133 Ibid.

134 Thos. F. Wilson to Hamilton Fish, 1 September 1870, Matamoros Despatches, RG 59, NA.

8: PRONUNCIAMIENTO, SANTIAGO TLATELOLCO, 20 AUGUST 1870

135 Leopold Morris, "The Mexican Raid of 1875 on Corpus Christi," *Quarterly of the Texas State Historical Association* 4 (1900-1901): 128-39; William M. Hager, "The Nuecestown Raid of 1875: A Border Incident," *Arizona and the West* 1 (Autumn 1959): 258-70.

136 Webb, *The Texas Rangers,* 255-90.

137 "Report of the United States Commissioners to Texas," *Depredations of the Frontiers of Texas,* 42d Cong., 3d sess., no. 39, 1-63; *Reports of the Mexican Committee of Investigation,* 127-63.

138 Wm. Steele to Richard Coke, 1 July 1875, *TFT,* 122.

139 Ibid.

140 John W. Foster to Hamilton Fish, 4 May 1875, *TFT,* 152.

141 Ibid.

142 John W. Foster to Hamilton Fish, 12 July 1875, *TFT,* 160.

143 Wm. D. Whipple to Adj. Gen'l., 2 July 1875, LR, AGO, RG 94, NA.

144 Ibid.

145 Mexico City *Two Eagles,* 28 July 1876; John W. Foster to Hamilton Fish, 12 July 1875, TFT, 160.

146 John W. Foster to Hamilton Fish, 7 July 1875, *TFT,* 160

147 Ibid.

148 Matamoros *Eco de Ambas Fronteras,* 8 October 1875, in LR, AGO, 1875, NA.

149 Endorsement, E.O.C. Ord, 4 October 1875, *TFT,* 120. The copy received from the *Eco* could not have been from the *Two Eagles* since Ord had it translated in San Antonio. See Mexico City *Two Eagles,* 1 September 1875.

150 Ibid.

151 Ibid.

152 Ibid. The translated proclamation was sent from Secretary of War William W. Belknap to Secretary of State Hamilton Fish. See Wm. W. Belknap to Secretary of State, 28 October 1875, *TFT*, 115. Originals of these letters can be found in LR, AGO (Main Series), RG 94, NA.

153 Ibid.

154 Ibid.

9: PRONUNCIAMIENTO, AZCAPOTZALCO, 18 MAY 1876

155 Michael C. Meyer and William L. Sherman, *The Course of Mexican History* (New York: Oxford University Press, 1987), 414.

156 Mexico City *Two Eagles*, 7 June 1876.

157 Thomas A. Wilson to Hamilton Fish, 7 July 1876, Matamoros Despatches, RG 59, NA; Richard Blaine McCormack, "Porfirio Diaz en las Fronteras Texana, 1875-1877," *Historia Mexicana* 5 (January-March 1956): 402.

158 John W. Foster to Hamilton Fish, 26 May 1876, *Report and Accompanying Documents of the Committee on Foreign Affairs on the Relations of the United States with Mexico*, 45th Cong., 2d sess., no. 701, 53; Mexico City *Two Eagles*, 31 May 1876.

10: PRONUNCIAMIENTO, HEROIC MATAMOROS, 27 FEBRUARY 1877

159 Thos. F. Wilson to Hamilton Fish, 7 July 1876, Matamoros Despatches, RG 59, NA.

160 Robert L. Robinson, "The U.S. Navy vs. Cattle Rustlers: the *U.S.S. Rio Bravo* on the Rio Grande, 1875-1879," *Military History of Texas and the Southwest* 15, 2:44-52; Michael G. Webster, "Intrigue on the Rio Grande: The *Rio Bravo* Affair," *Southwestern Historical Quarterly* 74, 2:149-64. Richard T. Marcum, "Fort Brown, Texas: The History of a Border Post" (Ph. D. diss., Texas Tech University, 1964), 199-201.

161 Thomas F. Wilson to William Hunter, 17 February 1877, Matamoros Despatches, RG 59, NA.

162 Ibid.

163 Ibid.

164 Mexico City *Two Eagles*, 10 March 1877; Thomas F. Wilson to William Hunter, 24 February 1877, Matamoros Despatches, RG 59, NA; John W. Foster to Hamilton Fish, 3 March 1877, *Mexican Border Troubles*, 45th Cong., 1st sess., 3.

165 Thomas F. Wilson to William Hunter, 28 February 1877, Matamoros Despatches, RG 59, NA.

166 Ibid.

167 Thos. F. Wilson to William Hunter, 10 April 1877, Matamoros Despatches, RG 59, NA.

168 Ford, *Rip Ford's Texas*, 413-14; Goldfinch, *Juan Cortina*, 63; John S. Ford, Memoirs, Baker Texas History Center, University of Texas at Austin, 1239-40.

169 Thomas F. Wilson to William Hunter, 10 April 1877, Matamoros Despatches, RG 59, NA.

170 Juan N. Cortina to Porfirio Díaz, 19 January 1878, A*rchivo del General Porfirio Díaz, Memorias y Documentos* (Mexico City: Editorial Elede, 1959), 28:147-48; Douglas, "Juan Cortina: El Caudillo de la Frontera," 125.

Appendix
CORTINA'S BROWNSVILLE RAIDERS

A

Abrego, Cecilio
Abrego, Ignacio
Abrego, Monico
Adame, Manuel
Arocha [Rocha], Manuel

B

Ballí, Jesús
Barrientos, Marcos

C

Cabrera, Tomás[1]
Cantú, Jesús
Carrillo, Encarnación
Casas, Antonio
Cervantes, Tranquilino
Chaves, Jesús
Carreón, Antonio

D

De los Santos, Miguel
De los Santos, Trinidad

E

Escamilla, Francisco
Espinosa, Antonio
Espinosa, (brother of Cedro)

G

García, Anselmo
García, Candelario
García, Juan
García, Severiano
Garza, Alejos
Garza, Florencio[2]
Garza, Juan
González, Anastacio
González, Yndalecio (Endesio)
Guajardo, Clemente

H

Herrera, Jesús

I

Ibarra, Marcelo
Ibarra, Matías

J

Juárez, Antonio

L

Lerma, Victor
Longoria, Juan Antonio (El Coyote)
Losa, Jesús

M

Martínez, Francisco
Medellín, Tenorio

O

Olivera, Francisco

P

Perea, Diego
Pozo, Manuel

R

Rodríguez, Antonio
Rodríguez, José
Rómulo, Evaristo[3]

S

Sánchez, Andrés
Sánchez, Matías
Sosa, Jesús

T

Tapia, Casiano
Tapia, Manuel
Tapia, Román
Tegles, Eligio
Treviño, José María

V

Vela, Alejos[4]
Vela, Alejos, Jr.
Vela, Juan[2]
Vela, Merced
Vela, Narciso
Villanueva, Merced (servant to Jesús Ballí)

Others:

Juan el Malo
Juan (coachman living in Matamoros)
Lázaro (servant to Jesús Ballí)

CORTINISTAS INDICTED IN THE DEATHS OF
JESÚS MONTES AND JOHN FOX

A

Adame, Gil
Aguilar, José María
Aguilar, Rosalio

B

Balcones, Pedro
Ballí, Francisco
Becerra, Francisco

C

Cadena, Bonifacio
Cadena, Santos
Cano, Eugenio
Cavazos, Martín

D

De la Garza, Pánfilo

E

Escobedo, Augustin
Espinosa, Pedro

F

Flores, Chino
Flores, Plácido

G

Gallegos, Eligio
García, Severiano
García, Vicente[2]
García, Víctor
Garza, Genovevo
Garza, Francisco Treviño
Garza, Hilario

Garza, Jorge
Gómez, Carpio
González, Alejos
González, Juan
Guerra, Florencio

H

Hernández, Severiano

L

Ledesma, José María de
León, Martín
López, Luis
Longoria, Hilario
Longoria, Macedonio

M

Medellín, Francisco
Medrano, Antonio
Medrano, Enrique
Millan, Francisco
Montalvo, Antonio
Montoya, Antonio
Munguía, Juan

S

Sosa, Jesús
Sosa, Manuel
Sosa, Pedro

T

Tampacuas Indians:
Andrés
Cano
Carlos

Faustino
Fernando
Francisco
Jesús
Juan
Manuel
Ojos Chiquitos
Rafael
Toro, Honorio
Treviño, Hilario
Treviño, Pablo
Treviño, Rafael
Treviño, Rosalino

V

Vela, Salvador
Villanueva, Merced
Villarreal, Emiliano
Villarreal, Leonardo

Z

Zamora, Teodoro[5]

Others:
Anastacio
Felipe
Olamites
Romano

1 Tomás Cabrera, Cortina's chief lieutenant, was lynched in Market Square by Texas Rangers and a Brownsville mob on 11 November 1859.

2 Florencio Garza and Juan Vela were found guilty of first degree murder in the deaths of Robert J. Johnson and Viviano García and hanged on 22 June 1866.

3 Evaristo Rómulo was hanged in January 1861.

4 Alejós Vela was killed in the attack on the Brownsville jail on 28 September 1859.

5 Teodoro Zamora was the Chief Justice of Hidalgo County (resigned November 1858) who commanded Cortinista forces at El Ebonal on 14 December 1859.

BIBLIOGRAPHY

MANUSCRIPTS AND ARCHIVAL COLLECTIONS

Bazaine, Francois-Achille. Papers. Genaro Garcia Collection. Benson Latin American Library, University of Texas at Austin.

Bell, Peter Hansborough. Papers. Record Group 301. Texas State Archives, Austin.

Brownsville, Tex.,
  Office of District Clerk
    Cameron County District Court Minutes (1849-1914).
    Marriage Records (1848-1912).
  County Clerk's Office
    Cameron County Commissioner's Court Minutes (1848-1862).
    Cameron County Deed Records (1848-1885).
    Cameron County Probate Minutes (1848-1912).
  Tax Assessor-Collector's Office
    Cameron County Tax Rolls (1848-1866).
  City Secretary's Office
    Brownsville City Council Minutes (1850-1859).

Camargo Consular Despatches. Records of the Department of State. Record Group 59. National Archives, Washington.

Cameron County Election Returns, Record Group 307. Texas State Archives, Austin.

Canales, J.T. Papers. Connor Museum. Texas A & M University at Kingsville.

Cortina File. Daughters of the Republic of Texas Library at the Alamo. San Antonio.

Despatches from the Mexican Consulate in the United States. Records of the Department of State. Record Group 59. National Archives, Washington.

Despatches from United States Consulate in Mexico. Records of the Department of State. Record Group 59, National Archives, Washington.

Eighth Census (1860). Cameron County, Tex. National Archives, Washington.

Ford, John S. Memoirs. Barker Texas History Center, University of Texas at Austin.
_____. Papers. Texas State Archives, Austin.

Guerrero Consular Despatches. Records of the Department of State. Record Group 59. National Archives, Washington.

Haynes, John L. Papers. Barker Texas History Center. University of Texas at Austin.

Heintzelman, Samuel Peter. Papers and Journals. Library of Congress, Washington.

Hidalgo County Commissioner's Court Minutes (1852-1912). Rio Grande Valley Historical Collection. University of Texas Pan American Library, Edinburg.

Hidalgo County District Court Minutes (1853-1912). Rio Grande Valley Historical Collection. University of Texas Pan American Library, Edinburg.

Houston, Sam. Papers. Record Group 301. Texas State Archives, Austin.

Kingsbury, Gilbert. Papers. Barker Texas History Center, University of Texas at Austin.

Letters Received. Adjutant General's Office. Record Group 94. National Archives, Washington.

Letters Received. Department of Texas, District of Texas, and the 5th Military District, 1865-1870. Adjutant General's Office. Record Group 393. National Archives, Washington.

Letters Received. Trans-Mississippi Department. Records of the Confederate War Department. Record Group 109. National Archives, Washington.

Leyendecker, John Z. Papers. Barker Texas History Center, University of Texas at Austin.

Lubbock, Francis Richard. Papers. Record Group 301. Texas State Archives, Austin.

Marriage Register. Immaculate Conception Cathedral, Brownsville, Texas. Catholic Archives of Texas, Austin.

Marriage Register. Matamoros Parish Archives. Matamoros, Tamaulipas.

Matamoros Consular Despatches. Records of the Department of State. Record Group 59. National Archives, Washington.

Mier Consular Despatches. Records of the Department of State. Record Group 59. National Archives, Washington.

Pickett, John T. Papers. Library of Congress, Washington.

Runnels, Hardin Richard. Papers. Record Group 301. Texas State Archives, Austin.

San Román, José. Papers. Barker Texas History Center, University of Texas at Austin.

Seventh Census (1850). Cameron County, Tex. National Archives, Washington.

Starr County Commissioner's Court Minutes (1852-1923). Rio Grande Valley Historical Collection. University of Texas Pan American Library, Edinburg.

Texas Adjutant General's Records. Texas State Archives, Austin.

Vidaurri, Santiago. Correspondencia. Archivo General del Estado de Nuevo León, Monterrey, Nuevo León.

Walter Daniel Miller. Papers. Texas State Archives, Austin.

BOOKS

Archivo del General Porfirio Díaz, Memorias y Documentos. 32 vols. Mexico City: Editorial Elede, 1959.

Bay, Betty. *Historical Brownsville: Original Townsite Guide*. Brownsville: Brownsville Historical Association, 1980.

Benito Juárez: Documentos, Discursos y Correspondencia. Mexico City: Secretaria del Patrimonio Nacional, 1964-69.

Camargo Baptism Records, 1764-1864. Corpus Christi: Spanish American Genealogical Association, 1989.

Camargo Marriage Records, 1764-1879. Corpus Christi: Spanish American Genealogical Association, 1989.

Castillo, Pedro, and Alberto Camarillo. *Furia y Muerte: Los Bandidos Chicanos*. Los Angeles: Aztlán Publications, 1973.

Chatfield, W.H. *Twin Cities of the Border and the Country of the Lower Rio Grande*. New Orleans: E.P. Brandao, 1893.

Coker, Caleb., ed. *The News from Brownsville: Helen Chapman's Letters from the Texas Military Frontier, 1848-1852*. Austin: Texas State Historical Association, 1992.

Cruz, Gilbert R. *Let There Be Towns: Spanish Municipal Origins in the American Southwest, 1610-1810*. College Station: Texas A & M University Press, 1988.

Dabbs, Jack Autrey. *The French Army in Mexico, 1861-1867*. Hague: Mouton and Co., 1963.

Daddysman, James W. *The Matamoros Trade: Confederate Commerce, Diplomacy and Intrigue*. Cranbury, N.J.: University of Delaware Press, 1984.

De León, Arnoldo. *They Called Them Greasers: Anglo Attitudes Towards Mexicans in 19th Century Texas*. Austin: University of Texas Press, 1983.

_____. *Mexican Americans in Texas, A Brief History*. Arlington Heights, Ill.: Harlan Davidson, 1992.

_____, *The Tejano Community*. Albuquerque: University of New Mexico Press, 1982.

Dobie, J. Frank. *A Vaquero of the Brush Country*. Austin: University of Texas Press, 1965.

Flaquer, Mirabel Miro, ed. *Catálogo de Documentos—Carta de la Collección Porfirio Díaz, Tamaulipas, Marzo 1876-Noviembre 1885*. 2 vols. Ciudad Victoria: Universidad Autónoma de Tamaulipas, 1985.

Ford, John Salmon. *Rip Ford's Texas*. Ed. Stephen B. Oates. Austin: University of Texas Press, 1963.

García, Cleotilde P. *Captain Blas María de la Garza Falcon: Colonizer of South Texas*. Austin: San Felipe Press, 1984.

García, Paul, and José María Sanchez. *Tamaulipas en la Guerra Contra la Intervención Francesa*. Mexico City: Sociedad Mexicana de Geografía y Estadística, 1962.

Goldfinch, Charles W., and José T. Canales. *Juan N. Cortina: Two Interpretations*. New York: Arno Press, 1974.

Gregg, Robert D. *The Influence of Border Troubles on Relations Between the United States and Mexico, 1876-1910*. Baltimore: Johns Hopkins University Press, 1937.

Grimm, Agnes G. *Llano Mesteñas, Mustang Plains.* Waco: Texian Press, 1985.

Hobsbaum, Eric J. *Primitive Rebels: Studies in Archaic Forms of Social Movements in the 19th and 20th Centuries.* New York: Fredrick A. Praeger, 1959.

Hughes, W. J. *Rebellious Ranger: Rip Ford and the Old Southwest.* Norman: University of Oklahoma Press, 1964.

Irby, James A. *Backdoor to Bagdad: The Civil War on the Rio Grande.* El Paso: Texas Western Press, 1977.

Jenkins, John H., ed. *Robert E. Lee on the Rio Grande: The Correspondence of Robert E. Lee on the Texas Border, 1860.* Austin: Jenkins Publishing Co., 1988.

Kearney, Milo, and Anthony Knopp. *Boom and Bust: The Historical Cycles of Matamoros and Brownsville.* Austin: Eakin Press, 1991.

Kearney, Milo, ed. *Studies in Brownsville History.* Brownsville: Pan American University at Brownsville, 1986.

_____, ed. *More Studies in Brownsville History.* Brownsville: Pan American University at Brownsville, 1989.

_____, ed. *Still More Studies in Brownsville History.* Brownsville: University of Texas at Brownsville, 1991.

Kératry, Le Cte. E. De. *La créance Jecker, les indemnités francaises el les emprunts mexicains.* Paris, 1868.

Larralde, Carlos. *Mexican American Movements and Leaders.* Los Alamitos, Calif.: Hwong Publishing Co., 1976.

_____. *Carlos Esparza: A Chicano Chronicle.* San Francisco: R & E Research Associates, 1977.

Lea, Tom. *The King Ranch.* 2 vols. Boston: Little Brown and Company, 1959.

McWilliams, Carey. *North From Mexico, The Spanish Speaking People of the United States.* New York: Greenwood Press, 1968.

Metz, Leon. *Border: The U.S.-Mexico Line.* El Paso: Managan Books, 1989.

Montejano, David. *Anglos and Mexicans in the Making of Texas, 1936-1986.* Austin: University of Texas Press, 1987.

Nance, John Milton. *After San Jacinto: The Texas-Mexican Frontier, 1836-1841.* Austin: University of Texas Press, 1963.

Parisot, P.F. *The Reminiscences of a Texas Missionary.* San Antonio: Johnson Brothers, 1899.

Pierce, Frank Cushman. *A Brief History of the Lower Rio Grande Valley.* Menasha, Wis.: George Banta Publishing Co., 1917.

Rayburn, John C., and Virginia Kemp. *Centuries of Conflict, 1821-1913: Incidents in the Lives of William Neale and William A. Neale, Early Settlers in South Texas.* Waco: Texian Press, 1966.

Rister, Carl Coke. *Robert E. Lee in Texas.* Norman: University of Oklahoma Press, 1946.

Reports of the Committee of Investigation Sent in 1873 by the Mexican Government to the Frontier of Texas. New York: Baker & Godwin, 1875.

Robertson, Brian. *Wild Horse Desert: The Heritage of South Texas.* Edinburg: New Santander Press, 1985.

Rosenbaum, Robert J. *Mexicano Resistance in the Southwest, "The Sacred Right of Self-Preservation."* Austin: University of Texas Press, 1981.

Schoonover, Thomas D., ed. and trans. *Mexican Lobby: Matías Romero in Washington, 1861-1867.* Lexington: University of Kentucky Press, 1986.

_____, ed. and trans. *A Mexican View of America in the 1860s: A Foreign Diplomat Describes the Civil War and Reconstruction.* Rutherford: Fairleigh Dickinson University Press, 1991.

Smart, Charles Allen. *Viva Juárez: A Biography.* New York: Viking Press, 1947.

Stillman, Chauncey Devereux. *Charles Stillman, 1810-1875.* New York, 1956.

Thompson, Jerry. *Mexican Texans in the Union Army.* El Paso: Texas Western Press, 1986.

_____. *Vaqueros in Blue and Gray.* Austin: Presidial Press, 1976.

Tilley, Nannie M., ed. *Federals on the Frontier: The Diary of Benjamin F. McIntyre, 1862-1864.* Austin: University of Texas Press, 1963.

Tyler, Ron. *Santiago Vidaurri and the Southern Confederacy.* Austin: Texas State Historical Association, 1973.

Vanderwood, Paul J. *Disorder and Progress: Bandits, Police and Mexican Development*. Lincoln: University of Nebraska Press, 1981.

War of the Rebellion: A Compilation of the Official Records of the Union and Confederate Armies. 128 vols. Washington: Government Printing Office, 1889.

Webb, Walter Prescott. *The Texas Rangers: A Century of Frontier Defense*. Austin: University of Texas Press, 1965.

Woodman, Lyman L. *Cortina, the Rogue of the Rio Grande*. San Antonio: Naylor Co., 1950.

Zorrilla, Juan Fidel. *Governadores, Obispos y Rectores*. Ciudad Victoria: University Autonoma de Tamaulipas, 1979.

ARTICLES

Baldridge, Lillian W. "Cattle Bandit Extraordinary." *Cattlemen* 34 (June 1947).

Bello, Ruth T., ed. "The Descendants of Feliciana Goceascochea and Juan José Tijerina as Declared by María Hilaria Guerra de Cavazos." *Journal of Hispanic Genealogy and History* (1990).

Champion, A.A., and Vivian Kearney. "Papers and Personalities of Frontier Journalism (1830s to 1890s)." In *More Studies in Brownsville History*. Brownsville: Pan American University at Brownsville, 1989.

Davenport, Harbert. "General José María Jesús Carbajal." *Southwestern Historical Quarterly* 55 (April 1952).

Dugan, Frank H. "The 1850 Affair of the Brownsville Separatists." *Southwestern Historical Quarterly* 61 (October 1957).

Gatschet, Albert S. "The Karankawa Indians." In *Papers of the Peabody Museum of American Archaelogy and Ethnology*, (1888-1904).

Glavecke, Adolphus. "The Story of Old Times." In W.H. Chatfield, *Twin Cities of the Border and the Lower Rio Grande*. New Orleans: E.P. Brandao, 1893.

Hager, William M. "The Nuecestown Raid of 1875: A Border Incident." *Arizona and the West* 1 (Autumn 1959).

Hingo, Don. "Texas' First Aristocracy: Robber or Robin Hood." *Houston Genealogical Journal* 7 (1989).

Hunter, J.T. "Captain J.T. Hunter Tells of the Cortina War." *Hunter's Magazine* 2 (November 1911).

McCormack, Richard Blaine. "Porfirio Díaz en las Fronteras Texana, 1875-1877." *Historia Mexicana* 5 (January-March 1956).

Morris, Leopold. "The Mexican Raid of 1875 on Corpus Christi." *Quarterly of the Texas State Historical Association* 4 (1900-1901).

Neale, William. "Centennial Oration by the Honorable William Neale." In W.H. Chatfield, *Twin Cities of the Border and the Country of the Lower Rio Grande*. New Orleans: E.P. Brandao, 1893.

Rippy, J. Fred. "Border Troubles Along the Rio Grande, 1848-1860," *Southwestern Historical Quarterly* 23 (October 1919).

Robinson, Robert L. "The U.S. Navy vs. Cattle Rustlers: The U.S.S. Rio Bravo on the Rio Grande, 1875-1879." *Military History of Texas and the Southwest* 15, No. 2.

Shearer, Ernest C. "The Carvajal Disturbances." *Southwestern Historical Quarterly* 55 (October 1951).

Thompson, Jerry. "The Many Faces of Juan Nepomuceno Cortina." *South Texas Studies* 2 (1991).

_____. "Mutiny and Desertion on the Rio Grande: The Strange Case of Adrian J. Vidal." *Military History of Texas and the Southwest* 12 (1975).

Vigness, David M. "Indian Raids on the Lower Rio Grande, 1836-1837." *Southwestern Historical Quarterly* 59 (July 1955).

Webster, Michael G. "Intrigue on the Rio Grande: The Rio Bravo Affair, 1875." *Southwestern Historical Quarterly* 74 (October 1970).

NEWSPAPERS

Brownsville
  American Flag
  Daily Herald
  Daily Ranchero
  Daily Ranchero and Republican
  Evening Ranchero
  Fort Brown Flag

Corpus Christi
  Nueces Valley
  Ranchero
  Weekly Caller

Dallas
  Dallas Herald

Galveston
  Galveston News

Houston
  Tri-Weekly Telegraph

Indianola
  Commercial Bulletin
  Indianola Courier

Matamoros
  Boletín
  Daily Ranchero
  Eco de Ambas Fronteras
  El Jayne

Mexico City
  El Democrata
  El Cruzado
  El Figaro
  El Monitor Republicano
  La Patria
  Two Eagles

New Orleans
  Daily Delta
  New Orleans Picayune

San Antonio
  Alamo Express
  Herald
  Ledger
  San Antonio Daily Express
  Texan

Santa Margarita
   Ranchero

St. Louis
   Missouri Republican

GOVERNMENT PUBLICATIONS

Journal of the House of Representatives, Eighth Legislature, State of Texas. Austin: John Marshall & Co.,
   1860.
*State Gazette Appendix, Containing Debates in the House of Representatives of the Eighth Legislature, of
   the State of Texas.* Austin: John Marshall & Co., 1860.
Steele, William. *Report of the Adjutant General of the State of Texas for the Year 1875.* Houston: A.C.
   Gray, 1875.
U.S. Congress. House. "Conditions of Affairs in Mexico." 39th Cong., 2d sess.
U.S. Congress. House. "Depredations on the Frontiers of Texas." 42d Cong., 3d sess.
U.S. Congress. House. "Difficulties on the Southwestern Frontier." 36th Cong., 1st sess.
U.S. Congress. Senate. "Hostilities on the Rio Grande." 36th Cong., 1st sess.
U.S. Congress. Senate. "Impeachment of Judge Watrous." 34th Cong., 3d sess.
U.S. Congress. House. "Report and Accompanying Documents of the Committee on Foreign Affairs on
   the Relations of the United States with Mexico." 45th Cong., 2d sess.
U.S. Congress. House. "Texas Border Troubles." 45th Cong., 2d sess.
U.S. Congress. House. "Texas Frontier Troubles." 44th Cong., 1st sess.
U.S. Congress. House. "Troubles on Texas Frontier." 36th Cong., 1st sess.

UNPUBLISHED MATERIAL

Douglas, James Ridley. "Juan Cortina: El Caudillo de la Frontera." M.A. thesis, University of Texas, 1942.
Graf, Leroy P. "The Economic History of the Lower Rio Grande Valley." Ph.D. diss., Harvard University,
   1942.
Irby, James A. "Line of the Rio Grande: War and Trade on the Confederate Frontier, 1861-1865." Ph.D.
   diss., University of Georgia, 1969.
Larralde, Carlos. "The Cortinista Movement, 1848-1876." Long Beach, Calif.
Marcum, Richard T. "Fort Brown, Texas: The History of the Border Post." Ph.D. diss., Texas Tech
   University, 1964.
Thompson, James Heaven. "A Nineteenth Century History of Cameron County, Texas." M.A. thesis,
   University of Texas, 1965.
Webster, Michael G. "Texas Manifest Destiny and the Mexican Border Conflict, 1865-1880." Ph.D. diss.,
   Indiana University, 1972.

Photo by Esteban Reyes, Jr.

Jerry Thompson, professor of history at Texas A&M International University, received the 1988 Earl Davis Award for his contributions to Texas Civil War history, and in 1989 was named to the prestigious Piper Professorship for outstanding scholarship and academic achievement. He is the author of eleven books and many articles in historical journals and magazines.

Other books by Jerry Thompson:

Desert Tiger: Captain Paddy Graydon and the Civil War in the Far Southwest

Warm Weather and Bad Whiskey: The 1886 Laredo Election Riot

From Desert to Bayou: The Civil War Journal and Sketches of Morgan Wolfe Merrick, editor

Westward the Texans: The Civil War Journal of Private William Randolph Howell, editor

Henry Hopkins Sibley: Confederate General of the West

Challenge and Triumph: The First 20 Years of Laredo State University

Mexican Texans in the Union Army

Laredo: A Pictorial History

Vaqueros in Blue and Gray: Mexican Texans in the Civil War

Sabers on the Rio Grande

John Robert Baylor: Texas Indian Fighter and Confederate Soldier

Texas Western Press

*gratefully acknowledges
the following endowment:*

The Mary Hanner Redford Memorial Fund

*which make possible
this and other issues of*

Southwestern Studies